THE GLORIOUS PRESENCE

by

JOY FULLER

DeVorss & Company
P.O. Box 550
Marina del Rey, California 90291

ISBN: 0-87516-449-8

Library of Congress Card Catalog Number: 81-65753

Printed in the United States of America
by Book Graphics, Inc., California

THIS BOOK IS DEDICATED
TO
JESUS CHRIST,
WHOSE LOVE
NEVER FAILS

ACKNOWLEDGMENTS AND INTRODUCTION

These true life experiences portray the fulfillment of Jesus' promises, when He said:

I WILL PRAY THE FATHER, AND HE SHALL GIVE YOU ANOTHER COMFORTER, THAT HE MAY ABIDE WITH YOU FOR EVER; EVEN THE SPIRIT OF TRUTH; WHOM THE WORLD CANNOT RECEIVE, BECAUSE IT SEETH HIM NOT, NEITHER KNOWETH HIM: BUT YE KNOW HIM; FOR HE DWELLETH WITH YOU, AND SHALL BE IN YOU. (John 14:17)

I WILL NOT LEAVE YOU COMFORTLESS: I WILL COME TO YOU. (John 14:18)

The bona fide presence of the radiant Jesus Christ is easily distinguished from present-day fraudulant impersonations by the brevity of His appearance, His intent, and the supreme message to the individual soul.

Our gratitude goes to those willing sharers who have been healed or set free by our Lord and Saviour—not in prayer meetings, not in church, not under mass hypnotic zeal—but quietly on a one-to-one basis.

This is a part of the Redeemer's work we hear very little about, but by which, if we but knew, He wins His thousands and His hundreds of thousands.

—The Editor

CONTENTS

HE'S STANDING BY ME
ALL THE WHILE

He's standing by me all the while;
He'd have me look to Him and smile,
To look away from doubt and fear,
And know that He is standing near.
And sometimes when the shadows fall,
I need to know that God is all;
No longer need I be afraid,
For Jesus is at hand to aid.

He's standing by me all the time;
It matters not the hour or clime;
I cannot falter, cannot fail;
His love forever will prevail.
I'll not complain, my lot bemoan;
I'll ne'er again think I'm alone,
For Jesus stands at hand to cheer
And have me know He's very near.

He's standing by me night and day;
I sometimes think I hear Him say:
"Just lean on Me and have no fear
And some good blessing will appear;
Just lift your thought to Me and know
That naught but Truth can e'er be so."
I always feel that I can try
When I know Jesus is nearby.

—Frank B. Whitney

Published by Unity School of Christianity, Unity Village, Mo.

CHAPTER 1

A WISH FULFILLED

HAVING EYES, SEE YE NOT? AND HAVING EARS, HEAR YE NOT?

—Mark 8:18

Being fairly new in a Study Group where we practiced meditation, I found that I had a few wrong concepts about Jesus Christ that were effectively straightened out by an inspiring and instructional dream. Perhaps sharing it with you may help others to realize that outer sensations are not important, it is the inner essence of Christ that counts.

One night our instructor related his account of another meeting in our area and of the success so many of its members had by experiencing various sensations. One girl, he said, even had a vision of the face of Christ.

Upon hearing this I thought, "How wonderful it would be to see the face of Christ!" But then I thought, Nothing like that would ever happen to me. Perhaps I am hopelessly unspiritual and am not progressing like other people." (I guess this is a question that haunts many people.)

After our meeting and meditations the following night and just before retiring I again bewailed my lack of outward sensation and wishfully thought that a vision of Christ would be the most sought-after experience I could ever have. Then came sleep and the dream.

In my dream it seemed I was walking down a very

1

ordinary street filled with tenement houses when I noticed a large crowd milling around one house in particular. I went over and asked someone what was happening. The members of the crowd excitedly told me that Christ was in there and was seeing people. When I asked if they thought He would see me they said, "Why don't you go in and see if you can get an appointment?"

Squeezing through the people I went up the steps and into an entrance hall where a man was announcing, "All those who are spectators step into the living room and all those who want appointments step into the dining room."

In the dining room another man recorded my name in a large book and told me that the Lord was in the kitchen and that they would call me when He was ready to see me. I could hardly wait. I was happy, nervous and excited at the prospect of this appointment with Christ. At last they called my name and told me to go through a swinging door where the Lord would meet me.

What would He be like? What would He say to me? What would I answer Him? These and more questions assailed me. In great anticipation I pushed open the door and entered a long kitchen where a table was heaped with all kinds of wonderful food.

But sitting at this table was not the Man I expected. Instead, there was a short, fat, swarthy and loudly jovial individual. He wore a long, dirty, food-stained white gown, had rough sandals on his feet and sported what looked like a four or five days' growth of beard. Obviously, this was not the Lord!

Trying to hide my disappointment I said, "Oh, excuse me, I was looking for the Lord and was told He was in here."

Cheerfully he jumped up from the table and held out his hand. "Glad to meet you, Joan," He said, "I'm Jesus."

Christ born anew in your heart

Then He invited me to sit down and share the meal with him. He stated the food was from the delicatessen, was absolutely delicious and was kosher. I was greatly shocked, but decided to make the best of the situation so sat down with him. His laugh was frequent and very hearty. I found myself enjoying this happy person (whoever he was) immensely. We laughed, joked, talked and exchanged morsels of food and sips of drink. Then He asked me if I was disappointed in Him.

I replied that I had honestly thought He would appear more holy or reverent, at which He slapped His leg, sat back and belly laughed. "Can't you see a guy going around like this all day?" He said, rolling his eyes upward and putting his palms together in a mock attitude of prayer. "What a bore!" He exclaimed. We enjoyed another good laugh over that one. "Let me tell you something," He said. "People who appear holy very seldom are."

For several minutes we talked more about this and joked and I realized I had developed by then a very warm and friendly feeling for this little, stout and jovial fellow. He then seemed to become more serious and asked abruptly, "How is your Study Group coming along?" "Pretty good," I answered and then He said, "Yes, I'd say you're all doing pretty good, too."

Then, as I watched, He stood up beside the table and slowly a change began to come over Him. He grew taller and thinner—His growth of stubble turned into a neat, auburn beard. His eyes grew wise and beautiful and the robe turned from a greasy garment into a glistening white covering. The beautiful Christ now stood before me. I was overwhelmed with shame and remorse for the very offhanded, friendly way I had treated Him. Covering my eyes with my hands I could no longer look at Him.

4

Then He asked, "If I had looked like this when you came in, would you have laughed and joked with Me and enjoyed My company so much?" I admitted that such would not have been the case.

Then He said, "Listen, I have something to tell you. Outward sensations, visions, miracles and even healings in themselves are of no real importance. The only important thing is the essence of the Christ in a life. LOOK FOR THE ESSENCE OF THE CHRIST IN YOUR LIFE."

With these words still ringing in my ears I woke up and could only exclaim, "Never again will I look for outward sensations or desire the experiences of others for myself. Henceforth, I will look only for the developing Christ Spirit in my heart and life."

MEDITATION

Sensationalism

Dear Lord,

There seems to be a pattern in human thought that decrees that in order for someone or something to be important it must be sensational. Help me, dear Lord, to keep clear of such thinking and to keep my thought centered on the worthwhile characteristics of people and things.

I would release the glamour of the outer world that would bind or strip me of dignity in Your sight. I know the sensations of the world will soon pass away, but my life with You will go on forever. I would look into the heart of matters and learn the lessons You have for me to learn. I am clear, calm and satisfied. Thank You, dear Lord.

Amen.

CHAPTER 2

GOD LOVES ME AND FORGAVE MY AWFUL PAST

THE WAGES OF SIN IS DEATH.

—Romans 6:23

BE OF GOOD CHEER; THY SINS BE FORGIVEN THEE.

—Matthew 9:2

Perhaps you were raised in a kind, loving family where your folks attended to your personal needs. I was not so fortunate. I grew up in the slums of a great city, carelessly unaware of anything but pleasing myself in the fastest and most expedient way possible. The end always seemed to justify the means as far as I was concerned.

Needless to say, wrong things led to bad situations and before I hardly knew it I was working for an organized gang of crooks. I was a bone breaker. If the company needed anyone smashed up or their bones broken, I did it.

My wife didn't know what I was up to. I earned the money and she was wise enough not to ask any questions. She later told me she had been praying for me because she felt something was definitely wrong. She didn't know HOW wrong!

The day I broke both legs of a man, the sole support of his wife and six children, I pocketed the money and considered it a satisfactory day's work.

As I stumbled down the sidewalk, half drunk, I suddenly felt two very firm hands upon my shoulders, straightening me up and turning me about-face. To my utter astonishment I came face to face with Jesus Christ.

Don't ask me how I knew Him. There is no logical reason how a sinner like me would ever recognize the most perfect man who ever trod this earth. But I was given to know who He was. Anyone would know Him! The stamp of divinity is plainly seen.

I sobered up instantly. His eyes sorrowfully looked deep into the depths of my soul. I felt as though a sword was being turned around inside me, laying bare all the secret sins of my horrible existence. My shame was unbearable.

Remorse overcame me. I wept right there on the busy sidewalk . . . I asked for forgiveness. I pleaded for another chance to make amends. I felt the burden that guilt places on a person when he has lived contrary to God's will and love.

Then I felt the soft warmth of the Lord's majestic, unjudging love steal over me. It began in my head and spread down to my toes until every part of me tingled with new life and new purpose. Joy was felt by me for the first time in my life. I had never known what it felt like to be truly happy until this moment. Just think, God could love even a sinner as bad as me!

No words can express how I really felt the day that Christ liberated me from myself and claimed me for His own. Ever since, I have lived for Him, placing God's will first in my life. Now that I know how, I find that living love into expression is the greatest and most exciting adventure anyone can experience. There is no end to the variety of opportunities God presents to us every day. In every challenge, there is a hidden way out that Christ provides. Life is a great big adventure! When I seek to find the RIGHT answers to problems now, I never cease thrilling at what I discover! And then when I use the Lord's way, there is another awe-shaking time of realizing God is using me as an example to teach others.

Needless to say, my wife was elated over all of this! She helped me in every way possible. We quietly left the area where I was known and moved to a distant state. I changed my name and tried to get work. All I could get was a cleaning job. But it is honest work and I manage to earn enough to just provide for us. We know now that there is something far greater than money can buy. The luxuries of this world hold no more appeal for us.

I know there is a heaven where Jesus lives. It is the place He said He was going to prepare for us. I want to be found worthy some day of living there with Him—if He will have me. I think He will because I know He loves me. He also knows I am trying my best to please God.

Since my conversion (and that is really what it was), my wife and I have opened our home to people in need of all kinds of help. We have prayer meetings at least once a week and try to bring the lost and wayward to Christ. It is easy for me to spot people who are in trouble since I was there once myself. I am often led to speak to strangers and encourage them to meet with us, or even to change.

The little we do is not much considering how much God has done for me. He brought me from the poor, wretched creature that I was to a loving, kind human being who has hope in the future as well as joy in the present.

I sometimes wonder how I must have looked to the people who passed me on the city sidewalk that day of days. Our Lord was probably not visible to them. As Jesus once said, "Their ears are dull of hearing, and their eyes they have closed." (Mat. 13:15) Thank God I can say with the blind man who was healed, "I *was* blind, *now* I see." (John 9:25) They doubtless thought I was a drunken bum and no one cared whether I lived or died, and then they went carefully around me. They would have been surprised, wouldn't they?

MEDITATION

Forgiveness

Dear Lord,

It is wonderful to know there is Someone who loves me that I can trust. I can confess to You and You will understand, regardless of how deep in sin I may be.

Today I come to You and fearlessly expose my shortcomings. I ask Your forgiveness. I ask Your help. I ask that You flood me with Your Spirit of love and heal me.

I cannot comprehend Your love. I wonder how You can love me the way I am. Yet You obviously do. You are the giver and sustainer of life and I am still alive, so You must still love me and have a purpose for my soul. Amazing!

Cleanse my inner self and cast from me the errors I have willfully entertained in my self-righteousness, or my self-indulgence. Humble me, Lord . . . change me . . . make my house sweet and clean. Make my mind and body pure and holy. Help me, Lord, to realize Your love, and make me wholly Yours forever.

Forgive my weaknesses, precious Saviour. I give my weaknesses as well as my strong points to You. I am wholly Yours because I know I can trust You. I can count on You to do Your very best for me.

Thank You, precious Lord.

Amen.

CHAPTER 3

FREE!

IF THE SON THEREFORE SHALL MAKE YOU FREE, YE
SHALL BE FREE INDEED!

—John 8:36

Do you have a habit you wish you had never made?
If so, I know exactly how you feel! I felt that way a few years
ago myself. But now I am free from the habit, praise God!

The change did not come easily or quickly. It was a slow,
agonizing process until the climax came one night in a totally
unexpected way. Life is full of surprises!

Before this difficult experience which I'm about to relate,
whenever I had other problems, I could easily connect with
God and win a victory. For instance, one time I lost my job.

That was a time when I needed to know God was with
me and would surely take care of my family and me. I
knew, too, that never one door closes but another one
opens. If I had lost one job—well, I reasoned, God is a very
rich Father. He owns all the jobs in the world. He wants
His children prospered and cared for; therefore, He would
see that I got a proper job. I kept my faith on this and,
sure enough, pretty soon a better job turned up. I was
very grateful.

One winter I got a virus and was sick in bed for a while.
But I kept knowing God owned all the life and strength
in the world and that He loved me. It made sense to me

10

that if He owned all the life in the universe and loved me, then He was surely going to give me the health I needed, and He did! I wasn't about to stop Him, either!

But in the meantime I had developed a habit. No matter how hard I tried to hold on to my faith in God's ability to always provide the right answer—I could not seem to break it. Perhaps I wasn't honestly ready to give it up yet. But I was working on it. I had others praying for me, too. Still that nasty habit of yearning for tobacco hounded me. I tried chewing gum and other alternatives, along with my prayers, but I just couldn't seem to shake myself free from it.

There was a period of a week and a half when I managed to say no to myself. That week-end I found tobacco I had forgotten I had, and that was my "Waterloo." Another time I quit for fourteen days and thought that time I might really make it. I threw all the tobacco I owned in the garbage can. But that night a friend stopped by and lighted up—and that was it for me!

Another time my wife and I went on a vacation and I left my habit at home, or so I thought! In the middle of the night I got up and drove thirty-five miles from our cabin on the lake to the nearest town just to get a smoke. It was sickening to be such a slave to anything!

Unless you have had the smoking habit you have no idea how binding it can seem. I knew it was not real in the sense that Spiritual Man never smokes like a chimney. And certainly God, in whose image I am made, never smokes. Can you imagine God with a cigarette in His mouth? But all the logical arguments I could think of did not appease my appetite one bit. I was getting a cough and I knew this was not a good sign, either. I tried every way I could think of, but *on my own* I just couldn't make it.

At last my freedom came in a most unexpected way. It

really came after I had almost given up hope. I guess I was down to my last second on the hope clock. I was reading my Bible and praying one night when I cried out in anguish, "Lord, heal me from this terrible habit!"

I had said, "Lord." I didn't even know whom I was addressing! It was the Lord God who made heaven and earth.

You can imagine my astonishment, when, in answer to my prayer, I saw my room slowly fill with a strange white light. It became brighter and brighter until I could hardly stand it. There, in all His glorious majesty, stood my Saviour, Jesus Christ.

He was looking right into me with the sweetest, most penetrating smile I've ever seen. He surely knew what I had been going through. I felt relief immediately.

I just wanted to melt into His love right then and there. It was tremendous . . . it was magnificent . . . it was overwhelming! My words are inadequate to describe the emotion I felt. Then He spoke and said,

"YOU ARE FREE FROM THAT HABIT!"

This was the simple truth! I was instantaneously freed from any further desire to smoke.

As suddenly as He appeared, He vanished. That was fifteen years ago and I am still free and marveling at the great love and compassion He has for us all.

Just think, He cares enough about us to make a special effort to set a man free from a silly habit like smoking. I suspect there are some habits and terminal illnesses we are not able to trust God to heal. They are strongly ingrained in human consciousness. This is when the Comforter of Jesus is especially needed and potent.

Since then I am alive in His love and it makes a big difference in my desires. I find I want to seek out and serve

God more in countless ways. I'm grateful, so very grateful. What He did for me, He will do for you, if you will only ask Him.

MEDITATION

Freedom

Dear Lord,

I know Your will for me is freedom and all goodness. I also know that what I do today affects my tomorrows. Help me to be alert and to live according to Your standards every day and not start something I can't finish. Little acts become habits.

Help me to be wise and on my toes, Lord, so that I will not begin a habit that might bind me later. Your strength will help me to say "No, thank you" when friends encourage me to do wrong.

When others try to make me feel out of place because I am not like all the rest, please strengthen my composure. Grant me confidence to smile and feel comfortable as I stand for what is right. Let me feel the thrill of being unique in a relaxed manner suitable to one of Your followers. Thank You, dear Lord.

Amen.

CHAPTER 4

OUR GUIDE THROUGH THE SNOW STORM

HE HATH SAID, I WILL NEVER LEAVE THEE, NOR
FORSAKE THEE.

—Hebrews 13:5

It was late November when a letter came from my aunt
saying Mother was bedfast and she could no longer care for
her. I was alone and had very little money as my husband
was in the armed service. Nor was I strong in body for I
was just recovering from major surgery. But God had a job
for me to do and He supplied the extra strength and help
necessary for a trip I shall never forget.

My niece, Vera, offered to go along and help me do what
we both knew was necessary—bring Mother back to California to live. Shortly after my aunt's letter came we were
both on a bus headed for Mother's, not knowing what the
following two weeks had in store for us.

When we arrived at Mother's house, she was so ill we
weren't at all sure she would be able to make the trip.
But we started preparations for it anyway. We sold everything in her house except bedding and a few groceries.
I had made a deal for an old car for one hundred and fifty
dollars down, with a postdated check for one hundred
dollars. At the time I did not even know how I would be

able to cover the check, but the seller agreed to hold the check until the date indicated. Then the needed gasoline stamps were issued by the Ration Board.

It was Friday, December 6, 1943, 5 p.m. and DARK! The car, if one could call it that, was loaded. Mother was half lying and half sitting in the back seat. My niece and I were at last ready for the 1700 mile trip. How long it would take or what obstacles we would meet, we had no idea.

Only a few miles were behind us when our first problem came—a flat tire! After daylight came, I changed the tire and knew that I would have to arrange to get other tires as the spare was no good at all. The Ration Board in that town was not open on Saturday, so I called the home of the officer in charge and he kindly came to the office and gave me orders for two tires. Then we continued on our trip—one I shall remember the rest of my life and be thankful that God does hear and provides every answer, no matter how large or small the need might be.

Our first experience with "God at the Helm" was when we drove on to what looked like a firm road, but it turned out to be very soft dirt. All four wheels spun and our car started to sink and almost stopped. Workmen eating lunch by the road side started to get up to come and help us, but God beat them to it. It was as though there was a mighty push on the rear bumper. On we went! I saw the men with an awed expression on their faces fall back to the ground as we pulled out and went on.

I will dispense with the minor helps from God. There are many I recall that took place during the next five days. The old car had so many exhaust leaks that we had to leave the windows down to keep enough fresh air in the car to breathe. Mother kept herself covered well to keep warm. Going up or down hill Vera and I had to hold the car in gear as it kept jumping out of gear. Going up a hill I had to push the gas feed to the floor and then pull the hand throttle for more power. We never once doubted the fact that we would arrive at our destination in good order.

Each time it was necessary to stop for gas, food or rest, Mother had to be carried by hand saddle to and from the car. But about the fourth day out Mother said, "I think I can walk this time," and she did. We only held her arms for support.

How grateful we were to have God attending to our every need. Neither of us knew until later years that we three independently were using the same little prayer, " 'Tis up to You, Father. You know our every need and will provide!" This was proven over and over again on our long trip to California, especially when we got as far as New Mexico. We decided to keep driving through Amarillo instead of stopping for the night. This saved us motel expenses as well as time.

They had just had a very heavy snowfall and from what we saw on the highway, I believe it must have been a blizzard. Snow was from eight to fifteen feet high on either side of us and only one set of tire tracks led forward.

The lights on our car were so dim I could hardly see. The night was very dark with no reflections of any kind. It became more and more difficult to drive as the miles passed. I seriously considered turning around and going back, but there was no place in which to turn around. All I could do was to go on. For a brief moment I was panic stricken. I really had to firmly remember, God had helped us before and He would again. So I prayed, " 'Tis up to you, dear Father; I am only human and can do only so much. You didn't bring us this far only to let us down

16

when we need your help most. Guide this car and GIVE US LIGHT!''

Unless one has been privileged to SEE GOD they will find this hard to believe. For just as I asked for guidance and LIGHT, HE APPEARED. Vera and I both saw the Lord walking before our car. Mother saw Him too. We saw the outline of His figure, cloaked in a long, dark, flowing robe. A hood covered His head. He must have been at least ten or fifteen feet tall and the size we needed. LIGHT, glorious *light* streamed from under His garments. I could not see His feet; only the great white path of LIGHT was there, lighting the entire road ahead of us and guiding us safely through the snow storm.

He stayed with us through the storm and perilous road. Just as the snow banks started to clear and the road became free from ice He vanished as quickly as He came! My thoughts were only, ''Thank you, God, for your protection and guidance!''

I have not begun to mention all the things God did for us on that trip. Once I lost my purse with our last ten dollars in it in a restaurant. The waitress kept it for me, knowing I would come back for it. Also, a gas station attendant gave us gas without stamps; a motel owner rented us a room for much less than the usual rate, and many more could be mentioned.

God provided money in time to pay off the postdated check and to pay back all the money I had had to borrow for the trip. God is so wonderful! How could I doubt it after this trip? It took us just seven days to complete this trip.

Mother recovered and is now eighty-eight and happily living with my older sister. I lost my husband and God brought me one of the finest men I have ever known,

17

needing a mother for his girls. My niece has also married and has a family of her own. She says that was OUR WEEK WITH GOD. To me it was our week with God on earth.

MEDITATION

Provision

Dear Lord,

You once said, "Fear not, little flock; for it is your Father's good pleasure to give you the kingdom." I am setting my faith on this. If You could care so lovingly for the little family in this story, and feed the multitudes and heal them, surely You will care for me and mine.

"'TIS UP TO YOU, FATHER; YOU KNOW OUR EVERY NEED AND WILL PROVIDE!"

Help me to remember this little prayer. You are always with me to supply whatever is needed in Your sight. Thank You, Lord.

Amen.

18

CHAPTER 5

THE IRON CURTAIN CAN NOT KEEP JESUS OUT!

WHERE TWO OR THREE ARE GATHERED TOGETHER
IN MY NAME, THERE AM I IN THE MIDST OF THEM.
—Matthew 18:20

A few years ago one of my relatives came to visit me from behind the Iron Curtain. Being of the same family I felt free to tell her about our wonderful religious life in America and the new dimensions of religious revival here. She listened to everything. But when I got to the part where the Lord has appeared to so many in various walks of life and of the miracles happening to people because of this, she dismissed it as hysteria of a bored society. She made clear that no one who had a difficult job to do in order to survive daily would be even interested in anything like these "fabricated stories." With that the subject was closed.

A year later I had the opportunity of traveling behind the Iron Curtain as a translator to a group visiting there. We were given opportunity to visit freely in schools and to observe their methods used in education there.

Our hotel was on a lovely square just overlooking the city's ancient cathedral. I was looking forward to attending the Sunday church service. However, I was told it had been cancelled. So I decided to go out of doors and pray quietly by myself.

As I stepped into the hotel elevator the young man who operated it began to talk. The door was closed and no one was there but the two of us. He told me he was going to tell me something he had never told anyone but his wife before. He said, "A few years ago I met Jesus."

I looked at him jubilantly for I remembered my relative's caustic remarks that anyone surviving in a difficult daily job would never be interested in Jesus. I had to travel thousands of miles on a business that was not mine, into a city I never would have visited, in order to find a frail, tall figure with glowing black eyes say this sentence in a country where survival is difficult: "I HAVE MET JESUS!"

Just then some other people got on the elevator and our conversation was cut short. When I got out I asked if I could visit him at his home so we could talk further, and he consented.

I saw him the next day with his wife in their one tiny room, where a bed, table, and stove completely filled up the space. During our conversation I found that he had been a poor country boy who was raised in a state boarding school which was a military academy. At that time his fondest dream was to become an army officer. After his training he was assigned a place in the army.

A few days before his induction he went to visit his mother. From the railroad station he had to walk a few miles through open fields to reach her home. It was night and quite black, but suddenly he became aware that the darkness of the sky was pushed aside and in a large oval glow of light Jesus Christ appeared.

The light became stronger and began to move closer and closer until He, himself, was enwrapped in the light and was standing face to face in closeness with the Lord.

"He was just standing and looking into me," he said.

20

"So much love was in His eyes, and such peace came over me that I can not describe it.

"Jesus lifted His hands and pointed at me three times. Although He did not talk, I understand that our whole world is going to change soon. There is not much time left.

"From that day on I have been blessed with discernment of thought. I can read everyone's thoughts and I find most people are doing just about everything they ought not to do. So many people go to church for many false reasons, pretending to be something they are not. Everyone should be in prayer and service and loving the other fellow human being. Instead," he smiled, "you know.

"Once in a while my intellect rebels against my Lord's way of life. Then I have to become humble and remember His love for me. What I earn is shared with my mother and the poor. Sometimes I question my own judgment for doing so. Then I feel Him beside me, strengthening me in my decisions and I know it is the right way. For it is He who wants me to serve and He loves us so much. Nothing is too much or too hard when I remember His will.

"What I would like to tell everyone is this: 'Stop your old ways and pray and serve God. The time is running short!' " As I parted from this young elevator man I was struck with the sincerity of his message. THE TIME IS RUNNING SHORT.

As I think back on the occasion I am filled with joy and gratitude. I experienced God's hand leading my steps, allowing me to meet and talk with one of His true servants whose earnest and deep Christian conviction shall always be a source of inspiration to me in a world where people so often do not do the things pleasing to the Lord. I praise God for this experience and the opportunity to tell others about it.

Believe

Dear Lord,

Forgive me. I am one who has doubted that You are the Christ. Now I know better. I am one whose life has been changed by the witness of this man. Protect and prosper him, Lord, and help him.

I am certainly blessed in living in a free country where I can believe as I wish. I know that this is not so easy for others. Bless our country, Lord, and all the countries of the world, that freedom to believe in You may prevail.

Thank You for being a patient Lord and allowing me to make up my own mind about You. I will strengthen my belief now by studying my Bible and contemplating Your holy presence. Thank You, Lord, for loving me before I even accepted You and for loving me always.

Amen.

CHAPTER 6

NO RESERVATIONS!

O DEATH, WHERE IS THY STING? O GRAVE, WHERE
IS THY VICTORY?

—1 Cor. 15:55

In 1956 the dear friend I lived with for so many years found a lump in her breast. Upon visiting the doctor and undergoing a lengthy examination she was told she had a malignancy.

"I'm making reservations for you tomorrow morning at the hospital," he told her. "You do not have very long to live, with that condition! You may have six months if you do not have this operation. You have a good strong body and with the operation, you should have several more years."

The news stunned her and she was at a loss as to just what to do. "Make no reservations for me now, Doctor," she murmured. "I want to go home and consider this and decide for myself."

"No reservations?" he expounded! "You are a most foolish woman. Go home, and before nightfall call me so I can get you a room and set up the operation!"

She thanked him for being concerned for her welfare. He was a good doctor and she knew he sincerely meant to do his best for her. But she wanted to pray about it and make her own decision.

She drove home like a robot. Her mind was almost a blank as she went into her bedroom and locked the door. She couldn't think; she could hardly pray; she could scarcely believe the terrible verdict—6 months to live unless she had an operation! What could she do with only six months? She had a full lifetime planned of service for God. Six months was hardly an opener.

Hour after hour passed as she prayed and meditated, asking the Lord Jesus Christ to guide her. What should she do? She didn't want to die of cancer. She knew of the dreadful anguish of others she had visited in this condition. "Please, Lord Jesus," she implored, "I have given my life to You. Certainly You are not going to let me die now. I know it is not God's will that I suffer and die—God is love, and love does not act that way. This is the false world picture, but the world has no real power. YOU are the only REAL power in the universe.

"Dear Jesus, You have overcome the world. Heal me now! Free me from this false claim of evil. There are not two powers, good and evil; there is only one power, one God, the good, loving, kind God. The God of perfect life and health."

Just then the church bell in our section of the city began to toll midnight and the voice of Jesus Christ spoke clearly and powerfully to her.

"I AM YOUR LIFE, HEALTH, AND STRENGTH, AND I AM PERFECT *NOW*." These were His beautiful, profound words. "Of course You are!" she responded. She accepted her healing then and there—without reservations!

However, matters got worse after that. This often happens after one has had a divine revelation. Perhaps the adversary tempts one to the utmost to try to dissuade and discourage healing. But she knew God's will for her was life, health, and strength! He had told her so and she stuck with her

24

faith. She entertained no reservations! Her mind was at peace and she was full of assurance that all would be well. In perfect trust she worked daily and at night slept like a baby in its mother's arms.

One day she suddenly noticed that the condition had become inactive! Her faith had been tested and had been found pure. What a joyous reward and what a victory for Christ! She praised and gave thanks continually as power poured in from on high. Gradually her health and strength built up and her vigor returned. She refused to be afraid. She was then able to do the work of several people. Years later she easily passed a medical examination for health insurance.

My friend lived for over twenty years after that in active service for the Lord. She was the channel of blessings and healings for many, many people. I am grateful I had the privilege of knowing her, living with her, and serving with her. She was faithful to God to the end and He was faithful to her.

I pray this may lead you to seek God's guidance in your life and affairs. His guidance varies with each person, but His will for you will be for your highest good, of this I am sure. "Love never faileth."

MEDITATION

Healing Trust

Dear Lord,

I have a problem and You know what it is. I pray now for guidance to right action and for the assurance and faith that is needed. I know that You are with me all the way and for this I am grateful. What is right for someone may not

25

be right for someone else. We are all different and You have the right answers for each one of Your children.

Help me to flow freely and fearlessly with the right answer You provide. If there are negative thoughts and feelings that I am not aware of that may be contributing to the cause of this illness, such as fear, distrust, unforgiveness, lust, hate, judgment, jealousy, hypocrisy, self-righteousness, malice, or persecution—help me to recognize them hidden in myself and help me to root them out forever.

Forgive me, dear Lord, for all past mistakes and for any present wrongs I am committing needlessly or purposely. Help me to change my ways and become right with You.

I am praying now, and I will continue to pray and talk with You. I will also hold clean, pure, and healthy pictures of myself in mind. I will seek and find Your precious love and I find that even now I begin to feel Your presence. A certain comforting tenderness sweeps over me and I am assured that all will be well. You make good out of everything. I know You will make good out of this experience and draw me closer to You. Thank You, dear Lord.

Amen.

CHAPTER 7

SEASIDE VISITOR

AS SOON THEN AS THEY WERE COME TO LAND,
THEY SAW A FIRE OF COALS THERE, AND FISH LAID
THEREON, AND BREAD. . . . JESUS SAITH UNTO
THEM, COME AND DINE. AND NONE OF THE DIS-
CIPLES DURST ASK HIM, WHO ART THOU? KNOW-
ING THAT IT WAS THE LORD.

—John 21:9,12

Thick evergreen trees clustered on the cliff beneath my bedroom window. They were decked with tiny droplets of water that sparkled in rainbow colors as the early morning sun sent its beams across the sea. I was the only guest and I could hear the two owners downstairs busily cleaning and packing away various items inns find necessary in order to cater to a summer clientele.

Quickly dressing and grabbing a granola bar I ran down the stairs and out the door to explore my new surroundings. The salt air blew playfully through my hair as I followed a deserted path along the cliff until it ended in a steep descent to a sandy cove. This secluded spot became my private Shangri-La for the next few days while I was on holiday.

"What a place for a picnic!" I thought. But I was all alone because the summer visitors had all gone home to get their children back into school.

The days were sunny and mild so I took my Bible and reading materials, along with the car blanket and some snacks, and settled in the cove for long spells of quiet contemplation. The peace and beauty of this lovely spot provided ample inspiration and each day I felt the cares of my busy counseling work drop away.

One golden day passed swiftly into another and all too soon it was time to think about packing up and going home. However, the day before I was to leave I ran out of food.

A trip to town appeared unavoidable. As I drove down the cobblestoned streets little signs came into view—Bakery—Fish Market—Clothier—Gift Shop, and others. Each came and passed as I turned the corner and looked for a place to park. What should I buy for supper? I had kitchen privileges; perhaps I should cook myself a real dinner before departing. Or was this necessary?

As I meditated a bit on this before getting out of the car I received a sweet yet strong impression. It was as though the Lord were saying, "WHY DON'T YOU GET A FRESH-BAKED LOAF AND SOME FRESH FISH? BRING THEM TO THE BEACH. I WILL MEET YOU THERE."

Logic always seems to enter and deter one, when interested in a divine inspiration. How absurd, I reasoned. Fish is no good raw and in all my visits to the quiet cove I had not seen even as much as the remains of a fire, or any fire wood for that matter. It had even occurred to me that fires might be prohibited.

With that, I reluctantly dismissed the thought and bought instead a ready-made sandwich and a bottle of milk. I would take these to the beach and enjoy watching the sun go down over the water. Little did I know what was ahead for me!

A half-hour later, with supper in hand I walked triumphantly along the little path that edged the bluff. As I neared the descent it seemed I could smell wood smoke.

I climbed down the cliff to the cove. Beneath a high slanting rock, nestled into a sheltered spot was a fire of coals, glowing invitingly. A huge log had been drawn up before it as if placed for one to sit and dine.

The sea softly beat upon the shore and my heart pounded in my throat. The Master's presence was so strong I could almost see Him seated on the log in front of the fire, awaiting my arrival. I knew then and there, even as did the disciples long ago on a beach in Galilee, that it was the Lord.

I could almost hear His blessed voice asking politely, "AND WHERE IS YOUR BREAD AND FISH, MY BE-LOVED?" It was obvious He had provided the fire and had waited to see if I would obey and bring the bread and the fish. He had tested my faith and I had been found wanting!

He had, as usual, done His part. He always does. How often had I neglected or ignored His guidance! How much better is it to err on the side of faith than the side of unbelieving!

I sat numbly down on the log before the fire and tried to compose myself. The thought that the vast, universal Christ should become so individualized and personal, filled me with new joy and wonder. This is the mystery of God and it was beginning to mark me for new understanding and new service to Him. Humbly I accepted His comforting presence and felt His peace.

It was then that I noticed a strange smell. It seemed to be the aroma of sandalwood. Leaning closer to the fire I found that the glowing coals were richly fragrant with this scent. Carefully I rescued a tiny piece of wood and, as I reverently held it in my hands, recalled that sandalwood is an Eastern wood. What was it doing on a New England shore? Sandalwood is heavy and difficult to float. What further proof was needed to know the presence of my beloved Lord and His ability to manifest anything according to His wisdom, need and purpose.

The fact that it was actually sandalwood was confirmed shortly thereafter when I happened to meet a wood specialist who expressed incredulity that it had been found on a New England beach.

As I think about the whole experience I still feel the thrill of our Lord's loving presence, His patient correction, His tender chiding and companionship. What a Glorious Presence He is and how precious is our relationship that has lasted to this day! I pray that you may do this also, for it is through obedience to God's direction that we discover sweet, inner communion (as well as outer) with our Lord.

MEDITATION

Quietness

Dear Lord,

Quiet me down and remind me of my manners. I have become too talkative, too chatty. Help me to seek out a quiet spot, even if it is in my own back yard. Help me to discipline myself to sit quietly there each day.

Stir my interest in things of the Spirit and place in my hands reading material that will be so inspiring I will not be able to part with it until it's read.

Often I talk so much I destroy something very beautiful. Sometimes it is a special thought someone else has shared with me that should be kept holy. I would like to honor and respect confidences.

I would also like to become so still I can listen and hear Your voice. I heard it once. Help me to hear it again and obey. The joy of obedience is something I want to learn and experience. Gather me close to Your heart, dear Jesus, and slow me down inwardly and outwardly. Thank You, Lord.

Amen.

CHAPTER 8

FREE FROM FEAR OF DEATH

I AM PERSUADED, THAT NEITHER DEATH NOR LIFE,
NOR ANGELS, NOR PRINCIPALITIES, NOR POWERS,
NOR THINGS PRESENT, NOR THINGS TO COME, NOR
HEIGHT, NOR DEPTH, NOR ANY OTHER CREATURE,
SHALL BE ABLE TO SEPARATE US FROM THE LOVE OF
GOD, WHICH IS IN CHRIST JESUS OUR LORD.

—Romans 8:38,39

Death was a mystery to me and I hated to see my Papa
slipping away from me into its clutches. I was unable to
release him because Papa and I had always been very close.
We had come, as a family, through many trials together.
But there was another reason why I did not want to see
Papa die. . . . I feared death!

I was a young girl alone, caring for him, and I had never
confided my fear to him. I felt very insecure as the days
passed and my aged Papa seemed to grow weaker and
weaker. I dreaded seeing him go and wondered how it
would leave me. Would I miss him beyond my ability to
bear it, I wondered? How would I ever be able to go on
without him? And I wondered about his well-being. Would
the Lord really take care of him? Or would he just go into
oblivion? These and many other questions crossed my mind
as each day found him successively more ill.

One night before retiring, I read my Bible and tried to

compose myself. I finally fell asleep in the wee, small hours of dawn. Then in the morning I was awakened by what seemed to be our precious Lord and Saviour, Jesus, appearing before me. He was seated on the side of my bed.

He was glorious in white raiment and a dazzling white light was all about Him. He was looking off into the distance as He talked with me, knowing at the same time that I was intently aware of His presence and what He was communicating to me.

In my wonderment He seemed to be giving me this message: "YOUR PAPA WILL BE LEAVING THIS EARTH VERY SOON NOW. YOU WAIT A LITTLE LONGER." Then He disappeared.

What a comfort this gave me, to be able to see the Lord and to have the reassurance that He knew Papa's condition and was going to take care of him! How grateful I was to know Papa was in His tender care. I felt a peace beyond what words can tell. I was able to resign myself to Papa's passing and release him. He did pass a day or so later.

But from what the Lord had communicated, He also gave me to know that I must stay here and work for Him. I had to wait until later. If I was faithful and glad to do His will, He would strengthen and guide me throughout the years to come.

Although I have faced many serious problems since then, I have felt His presence helping me through. Whether it was a health problem or a lack of funds, or just loneliness— he has always brought me just the right kind of help each time.

I thank the dear Lord that He spoke to me that first day. His love has stayed with me all these years. My Papa has long since passed on into his peace and I believe that when my turn comes, I will also have the Lord's presence to help me make the transition an easy one.

Jesus Christ said, "Lo, I am with you alway, even unto the end of the world." (Matt. 28:20) I believe in every promise the Lord has given for reward to those who serve Him and when I play our church organ I sing in my heart: "Thank You, God—! Thank You, Lord Jesus Christ! Thank You!" The words of our Bible are true: "HE WILL SWALLOW UP DEATH IN VICTORY: AND THE LORD GOD WILL WIPE AWAY TEARS FROM OFF ALL FACES." (Isaiah 25:8)

MEDITATION

Comfort

Dear Lord,

My loved one has passed from my view. It is as though he has boarded a ship that has traveled far out to sea and has gone beyond my horizon line. I can see him no longer, but I know he is safe with You. In this I am comforted.

Each consciousness earns its own reward. He loved You, Lord. We are drawn to our own. Let this be my meditation, then. And let me be comforted in the awareness that life is without end. There is no separation in love.

Safe and secure, my loved one has found his home and I have found my peace in You.

Amen.

34

DON'T TELL ME YOU ARE THE CHAIRMAN OF THE BOARD!

I KNOW WHOM I HAVE BELIEVED, AND AM PER-
SUADED THAT HE IS ABLE TO KEEP THAT WHICH I
HAVE COMMITTED UNTO HIM.
                              —2 Timothy 1:12

It is exciting to realize how carefully the Lord works with each one of us individually. Being a well-trained psychologist I had the opportunity to see the advantages of half-way houses. Our community had none and the possibility of a great compassionate work struck me with such force I prayed about it. It soon became evident that the hand of the Lord was on me and that He was inspiring me to establish a half-way house to help those coming out of institutions adjust to ordinary life again.

It was not long before I located a large 16-room house available for rent in the city. When I contacted the owner, however, he wanted a very high rental. I was shocked at the price he was asking and slowed down in my enthusiasm. He told me that if I wanted the place I would need to sign a year's lease the next morning.

I took it to the Lord in prayer and told Him I felt the rent was outrageous since I had almost no capital of my own and only two sure patients. I fully expected Him to instruct me to forget the whole thing. To my amazement I heard Him say:

"ARE YOU WILLING TO DO IT FOR ME?"

I quickly responded, "Certainly, Lord! Certainly, I'll do it!" I thought about that. Doubt crept in. The adversary was really trying to discourage me and I hesitated on the excuse that I had so little money and so few patients I could really count on to pay their way. As the day continued I prayed again about it. Perhaps I had not heard Him correctly the first time. I had better ask again. So I did.

Then the Lord came to me and I heard Him say:

"WILL YOU DO IT *ALL* FOR ME?"

I hastily replied, "Well—yes—yes, I will—but I think—yes—I will!" It was a very restless night that followed and I got almost no sleep.

Morning came almost before I knew it and I still had grave misgivings. An hour before the owner arrived for me to sign the lease I again sought the Lord in prayer. I prayed something like this: "I know You are with me, Lord, and I know I can count on Your guidance in this. I want to do what is right and good BUT I certainly don't want to get myself into a big mess! What is Your will, REALLY, Lord?"

Then I heard His clear voice saying to me:

"WILL YOU GIVE EVERYTHING TO ME? YOU LOVE ME, DON'T YOU? WILL YOU DO IT FOR ME?"

I could not deny His clear voice or His clear question. And I could not deny that I loved Him, because I did. Hesitantly I replied, "Well—" and then I reached a point of decision—a point of no backward turning. "YES!" I replied. "I will do it and I will do it ALL for you!"

"THEN GO AHEAD AND SIGN THE LEASE," He patiently instructed.

I did sign the lease and within three months the house

was full. It was amazing to experience the flood of help that came from all directions at once. I took care of all the counseling, directing and business. My fiancée did the cooking and cleaning. Funds came from unexpected sources. Donations came in from friends and people interested in helping those less fortunate than themselves.

Young people, full of compassion and with a desire to serve, offered their services at a minimum wage just for the opportunity of helping others. The patients and their loved ones expressed gratitude. One by one our patients recovered and went out into the world, stronger and wiser and happier for having had the experience of our half-way house.

Within a year, a second house was added to the work. Then a third! The Lord really knew how much this service was needed. Business was booming!

Many interesting things have happened since I began our "Rehabilitation Center." Many good lessons are being learned both by patient and counselor.

I have learned to teach self-discipline, honesty and respect—for a few things. We expect our patients to be respectful of themselves, those around them and the people in charge.

Regarding this, our second client on the fifth floor was asked to move to the third floor where we could check him more carefully. He objected to my request, saying I was only the counselor. He asked to speak to the Director. I told him I was the Director. He asked to speak to the President of the Company. I said I was the President of the Company. Rather exasperated he said he would speak to the Chairman of the Board. Then he stopped short and looked at me. His chin dropped in dismay as he said, "Oh, no! Don't tell me YOU are the Chairman of the Board?" I laughingly admitted that I was, and that settled that!

It later dawned on me how much responsibility the Lord had placed on me, and how much He was depending on me to fulfill the needs of His people.

I am so grateful to know that Jesus sent His Holy Comforter to be with us even as He promised He would do. I can turn to Him night or day and find strength, direction and assurance. With God, I can not fail!

MEDITATION

Selfless Service

Dear Lord,

I have been shopping around in the wrong place for quite a while, it seems. I have been spending a lot of time in the self-service places when I should have been in the SELFLESS-service places. I'm sorry. Much time has been wasted.

Help me now to reorient my thoughts and emotions so that when a new project presents itself my first thought will be on how best I can serve YOU—rather than how best can I serve myself!

I realize there are many in this world who can benefit by the gifts You have given me. I realize that my own soul estimate will grow as I begin to function on a plane of service for You.

This does not mean I must resign my job and look for a place in a service organization, necessarily. It does mean, though, that wherever I am, I can shift the emphasis of my thought from self-gain, to service for God.

This does not mean I must leave my family every evening and go out and play my accordion or build a program of free services, either. This may be the right thing to do, but on the other hand, it may be right to just freely share wherever I am and whatever I do. Sometimes service begins at home, or with a loved one. Many a person who was called to be a missionary has found a need to be filled without leaving the country or even leaving his own home town or own home.

I pray that I may be receptive to Your guidance and that I may obey it. That will be sufficient, I am sure, to get me on the selfless path of service and insure true and lasting happiness. I listen now, dear Lord, for Your instructions. Thank You.

Amen.

CHAPTER 10

THE PROTECTING PRESENCE

YEA, THOUGH I WALK THROUGH THE VALLEY OF
THE SHADOW OF DEATH, I WILL FEAR NO EVIL: FOR
THOU ART WITH ME.

—Psalm 23:4

I don't remember seeing the sky brilliant with so many stars. It was a clear, summer's night. The moon was full and round and shed so much light it almost seemed like daylight. I could sense life about me and I was very resonant to it. The white beach gleamed in the moonlight. Shadows of trees and shrubs silently wove a pattern on the sand. Joyously, like a little child almost, I ran across the sand dunes, so full of life I could have taken flight, or so it felt! There was so much for which to be grateful. Breathless from running and almost overcome by the beauty of it all, I settled in a heap on a grassy mound and meditated on God. It felt so good to be there!

After the evening meal, the campfire was put out, and we went to our tents for the night. My companions went to sleep, but I lay wide awake still marveling at the night and listening to all the sounds I could hear. The calm ocean lapped against the shore smoothly. All was so peaceful. There seemed to be an unnatural stillness outside.

This moment was then filled by the awesome and powerful Christ Presence which appeared as though standing in the doorway of our tent. I was spellbound. I couldn't move or speak. I felt myself completely absorbed in the goodness of this great Being of Light. I had no fear, only love and awe. Time ceased; sound ceased; and we were one.

Suddenly, there was unleashed outside a tremendous roaring wind. The calm ocean became a sea of energy that tossed waves up on the shore line with force. Sand whirled up; our tents were uprooted from the ground and sent rolling down the beach, cots, sleeping bags and persons all inside. Over and over it rolled us until it stopped several yards down the beach as suddenly as it began.

All the time I was laughing. I could only feel happy and released. There was only joy and humor in the situation because I knew with assurance we were divinely protected, safe from any harm.

There was no difficulty getting out of the tent, but one family member could not find his glasses. Under usual circumstances they should have been lost or smashed, or both. But there they lay, neatly folded, unharmed, at his feet!

I feel a deep sense of awe and gratitude whenever I think of what happened. In the gale that had arisen, our tent might have blown away, leaving us stranded for housing or even hurt. But not a hair on our heads was harmed! The Christ knew our need and had answered it even before we called. Wherever we go I remember this—God is with us.

In the midst of the tempest, God is there! He is the calm spot of light and when we unite with Him we are safe always.

MEDITATION

Protection

Dear Lord,

What a good feeling it is to know You are protecting me night and day, You are here and I am safe in You. However, I will not take needless chances. I will continue to take wise precautions at all times. If I do my part, You will do the rest.

It is wonderful to know God's power is all around me. Help me to remember this and to share this information with others. Help me to give them the assurance that they can also look to You for help and security.

The world is kind of shaky these days, dear Lord. Many are seeking frail crutches to lean upon. They make believe they are safe and place their reliance upon wealth, power or prestige. Some even rely upon drugs to take their mind off their troubles, but all this is temporary. There may come a time when all this is taken away and they will have nothing left to depend upon.

Dear Lord, I know we cannot take things with us when we leave this world. And I know things in themselves cannot make me strong and secure. This comes from the Spirit of God within me. I pray to develop a stronger awareness of God's Spirit with me. Dear Jesus, I thank You for preparing the Holy Ghost so that Your Father's Spirit may be one with me. I am safe and secure forever!

Amen.

CHAPTER 11

SWEET GARDEN OF PRAYER

COME UNTO ME, ALL YE THAT LABOR AND ARE
HEAVY LADEN, AND I WILL GIVE YOU REST.
—Matthew 11:28

> There's a garden where Jesus is waiting,
> There's a place that is wondrously fair . . .

I have often wondered if the author of this lovely lyric,
Eleanor Allen Schroll, had an experience similar to mine.
It was in a beautiful Eastern garden in a night-time vision,
where I first met Jesus.

Despondent and sad in my life of servitude and many
beatings received from the man of the house where I did
menial labor, I sought relief. I lifted the latch and opened
the huge gate in the wall surrounding the wondrously fair
garden. The place was not unfamiliar for I had been there
many times before. It belonged to the palatial home where
I worked.

There were enclosures made of stone for the green shrubs.
Cool fountains played in their twilight setting amid rare
flowers now cloaked in the shadow of dusk.

I walked on the well-kept paths, gazing at the beauty
surrounding me; I welcomed the tranquility of this place.
Then, as I knelt in prayer, I felt the gentle breeze of
evening drying my tears and soothing away the anguish of

the day. To this place, glowing with the light of His presence, I had come with my burdens and cares.

The palatial, white house stood at one end of this cool, quiet garden. Above its stately columns, hung with vines, rose turrets and towers. From behind the first roof there rose a magnificent dome capped by a graceful spire. Above the spire in the light blue sky was the face of Jesus Christ in living colors. His splendor filled the heavens above the dome and a glorious white light flooded everything.

He looked deep down into the depths of my soul and I was touched and healed of my misery by His tender, compassionate love. It seemed He was lifting a very heavy load from my weary body.

I rested and let His peace enter my mind as His words came to me, "Come unto me—I will give you rest."

He came to me then when I needed Him and He has come to me since then. Many challenges have come my way, but I know I can always count on His never-failing help whenever I enter that beautiful Garden of Prayer.

MEDITATION

Rest

Dear Lord,

Tonight I feel weighted down with problems. I seek You for relief. You experienced every human problem possible to man so You must know how I feel. I would rather talk with You than go to bed, although I'm dog-tired.

I know my problems are more than physical. Enter my mind and heart, dear Lord. Heal my emotions. Help me to forgive others. Help me get rid of hurt feelings if I feel

M. RUSSELL

GOD IS LOVE

picked on. The work must be done. I know all work is for Your glory when it is done with a right attitude.

I am grateful for my capability in this work, dear Lord. Help me to work graciously with all others and give me the strength and courage to carry on. May I remember to take quiet times to balance my life between rest and motion.

I would live each moment in Your restful presence whether I am working, resting or playing. Here I am, Lord. I release myself and all that concerns me to You. Take me. Use me, and help me to bring light and cheer to others.

I feel better now for having talked with You. Thank You for Your patient and understanding love.

Amen.

CHAPTER 12

ASCENDED MASTERS, MEDIUMS AND SPIRIT GUIDES? "MY LORD AND MY GOD!"

MULTITUDES, MULTITUDES IN THE VALLEY OF DE-
CISION: FOR THE DAY OF THE LORD IS NEAR IN THE
VALLEY OF DECISION.

—Joel 3:14

I was seated near the platform looking up at the speakers as each one expressed his religious views to the gathering. There must have been close to a thousand young people assembled. They came from all over the United States and Canada. The festival was not unusual; there are a lot of such gatherings going on these days with many voices and much running around and a lot of confusion.

I listened to many different beliefs. Some speakers were mediums and contacted relatives beyond the grave. Some gave messages from ascended masters. There were psychics who told people about their past and spoke of spirit guides.

I had come to this convention in a state of confusion and was becoming more confused by the minute. As a child I had been raised in a Christian Church, but it had faded into the past. I married and was now out looking around for perhaps something new and more exciting than the old way. I was looking for something that would capture my fancy

47

and stimulate my faith in God. I always believed in God, but I felt a need to exercise new dimensions in my thought about Him.

As I studied the various speakers on the platform I felt drawn to one in particular. She seemed earnest and sincere and spoke from within her heart the conviction she held of Jesus Christ as her Master and Saviour. I decided she might have some knowledge from which I could benefit.

It was announced that certain selected speakers would participate in a laying on of hands ceremony that afternoon. I decided to present myself before this particular Minister and request her blessing. As the time came for prayers I walked directly up to her, hoping with all my heart for a definite answer to my need for spiritual awakening.

I did not have long to wait. As she placed her hands upon my head the Spirit of God that had so long slumbered in my soul began to stir into action. I felt a great charge of spirituality enter my mind and body. I felt exalted and tingled from head to toe. A delightful sense of peace and well-being entered me. I felt at the moment very glad, with an unsure sense of just why I felt this way.

As the line moved on I felt the need for more reassurance and more understanding. It seemed like a door had been opened a crack and I had had an opportunity to peek inside, only to have it closed, leaving me wondering and fearful again.

That night when I went to bed I turned and tossed and could not sleep. My mind was so confused I didn't know what to think. I prayed that God would take away my sleeplessness and confusion and let me know the truth once and for all.

Then it happened in a flash! There He was, Jesus Christ, standing bathed in light by my side, with His blessed hand on my left shoulder. His face was full of love and so youthful. His neat beard was auburn and His robes were of radiant white. It was as though He was saying to me what He had said to Thomas, His disciple, long ago. Thomas had not been with the other disciples when Jesus had appeared to them after His days in the tomb. Thomas doubted that Jesus had died and had risen from the dead.

Jesus entered the room, our Bible tells us, although the doors were closed and locked for fear of the Jews. Jesus entered my bedroom in the same way, without opening a door or window. He just appeared. And He was telling me a similar message as He had told Thomas. The account is found in the Gospel of John, Chapter 20, verse 27:

"REACH HITHER YOUR FINGER, AND BEHOLD MY HANDS: AND REACH HITHER THY HAND AND THRUST IT INTO MY SIDE: AND BE NOT FAITHLESS, BUT BELIEVING. AND THOMAS ANSWERED AND SAID UNTO HIM, MY LORD AND MY GOD!"

There is a famous painting of Jesus knocking at the door of the heart. He does not use outer doors, He uses inner doors! I had opened the door to my heart and He had come in to me.

In the 24th Psalm we read: "Lift up your heads, O ye gates; and be ye lift up, ye everlasting doors; and the King of glory shall come in. Who is this King of glory? The *Lord of hosts,* he is the King of glory." It was very clear to me who the King of glory was and is. None other than Jesus Christ! Lord of all the lords, and King of all the kings! Praise God I know the truth that makes me free from any further confusion!

The King is here, visible or invisible, in the midst of the religionists, mediums, psychics and the many varied religious practices and beliefs. He is at work, touching and calling His own to new life and faith, and I have fellowship with the multitudes who belong to Him.

MEDITATION

Spiritual Strength

Dear Lord,

In these days of mass confusion, I cling to You. You are the Lord of all lords and the King of all kings and You are sufficient. I adore You and I love to serve You.

Through my union with You, I am strengthened in the good purposes I want to accomplish. I know I cannot do them alone, but with Your power backing me up, I can be successful.

It is a great comfort to feel Your stabilizing effect as I stand solidly on my faith in God Almighty, and His beloved Son, Jesus Christ. I know what I believe and I live by it and join and support others of like mind. I also help others of doubtful mind to understand the true King and Master of us all. In love and compassion I share, without proselyting, the truth that I know.

Amen.

CHAPTER 13

GIVE THANKS!

O LORD MY GOD, I WILL GIVE THANKS UNTO
THEE FOR EVER!

—Psalm 30:12

My husband and son were out for the evening. I was
seated alone at the kitchen table eating dinner when suddenly, out of nowhere it seemed, a deep, ageless voice like
God's spoke and said:
"DO YOU EVER GIVE THANKS TO GOD?"
I was so shocked I dropped the fork I was eating with and
began to shake. Surely it must have been God because no
one but God knew my secret sin. I never gave thanks to
God and I never gave thanks to anybody! I just felt uncom-
fortable saying "Thank you."

It seemed to me that this was a very unnecessary custom
and I didn't like it. Surely God knew I was grateful, so why
should I bother to thank Him? As for other people—well—.

One time a friend had given me a portrait of her little
girl. The child had attended our camp on the lake as a
baby while her daddy did some work for us. We had
watched this child grow up and really thought that if we
ever had a daughter we would like a girl just like this one.
When she gave me the picture I had looked at it quickly
and then changed the subject. I just didn't want to have to
say "Thank you."

51

Another time an acquaintance invited me to her home on the shore. I went and had a great time. But when the hour came to leave, I ducked out hurriedly. I didn't want to have to stand there and thank them. Furthermore, they might have expected to come and visit us in return and that would have been a real chore as they had several children.

When God spoke to me that evening I felt the presence of a very great love and a feeling of tremendous wealth. It was almost as though I had the whole world to give away! It was all mine to give! What a feeling! I can't explain it but I wanted to just give and give to make up for all those years of stinginess.

The idea that I could have been so petty as to have withheld a large or small "Thank you" appalled me. I was changed from a selfish, greedy person into a loving, grateful, sharing person and I loved the feeling. It felt SO good! What a relief not to have to hide or run away from something. I could just be open and free-flowing, generous—and still have plenty.

The next morning it seemed as though the trees were saying thanks to the breezes that blew their boughs. The flowers were saying thanks to the sunshine and the birds were saying thanks to God for their breakfast. This gave me an idea to say grace.

First of all, I had to explain to my husband and son all that had happened to me the night before. I told them my secret and how God had healed me from my greediness and inconsiderateness. I also told them I was sorry for having been so stingy and selfish all those years. They understood. They knew God had changed my life and accepted it.

I then gave the first grace ever said in our house at the breakfast table that day. The spirit of humility and gratitude was present in all of us and a lovely reward came because of it.

As I began to say a humble prayer of thanks for our good night's rest and the supply of good food and help for the day, there appeared before us the eyes of Jesus Christ. He was looking directly into mine. He smiled a knowing smile as my husband and son watched Him with me. Brows, forehead, nose, chin and mouth took form before us and we felt His blessing on us and our home.

I say "Thank you" now, and I will continue to say it forever. The Lord of goodness is with me and with my family as we thank Him each day. What a good God we have. He fills my cup to overflowing, even as He does yours. I count it a privilege and a joy to say, "THANK YOU, GOD!"

MEDITATION

Gratitude

Dear Lord,

How easy it is to accept Your gifts and forget to say, "Thank You!" But I'm sure You like to be thanked and appreciated. I do. Praise should be natural to man, but we somehow depart from naturalness.

As I observe Your birds, Lord, I hear them give thanks to You each morning when they wake up. It is very early, but they are on the job! They must do this before they do anything else!

They give You thanks and praise at evening, too. I love to listen to their carols at twilight. What a blessed way to go to sleep, giving thanks to our Creator.

I am going to be more appreciative of You, Lord. I am going to thank You every time something good comes my way—beginning right now. Thank You, dear Lord, for being my Saviour and my Teacher and my Protector. Thank You for Your great love and for Your provision for me over the years. Thank You for your help this day. May I prove my worthiness as I recognize You in the midst of my life and affairs.

Amen.

CHAPTER 14

THIS IS MY HEALING!

JESUS CHRIST MAKETH THEE WHOLE!

—Acts 9:34

Jesus said in effect that if we are to be "The Light," we must bear witness to "The Light." Herein is my witness.

I had just passed through possibly the most difficult period in my life in which for many months I had watched a man, a home and a work disintegrate. Though I am not unfamiliar with the Truth, to my human sense all I could do in this situation was to stand by with a freeing, releasing love. At the culmination of the experience I was without employment.

Surely God was very nigh, for within a matter of days I was assigned to a new position and a brief period of vacation allotted to me that I might visit my family prior to embarking on my new work.

This time with my loved ones was a joyous and healing experience and was to bring with it also a challenging experience. On the day before my scheduled 860-mile drive to start my new work, I had a terrific fall.

I bring to recollection the pain and the fear of those hours following my fall and the subsequent long drive to my place of employment only to enhance the story of the miracle healing which took place through the power and the love of Jesus Christ.

Without any doubt in my mind there was a dislocation in my back. I could not bend over without great pain and when I sat down it seemed in the very process that the bones of my knees grated together. However, through prayer and tenacity I managed to carry on for about a week.

I believe in miracles. I believe that we are to take the promises of Jesus Christ at face value. "Ask and ye shall receive," He said, and I asked for healing. I had asked in faith and I gave thanks for this healing in advance.

Up to this point the outer experience was the same—the experience of pain and discomfort—but I KNEW the healing had already taken place. I reasoned that not all miracle healing is feeling. It can be, of course, but perhaps it is sometimes the striking at the root cause of the pain. (The many cases at Lourdes point that out.) I knew I must take the recipe that Jesus Christ gave us and stick to it. "Whatsoever things you desire, when you pray believe that you have it." Believe it before you see it! Believe it before you feel it! Believe and act like you already have it! Deny the pain; affirm the healing.

"Father, we thank thee that thou hast heard our prayer." The essence of the desire and the need is the real prayer.

Then came a night when I awakened in excruciating pain. I heard my own voice crying out to the pain: "You are NOT of God!" And then softly I heard God whisper, "Anything you ask in My Name." Then the indescribable experience happened!

I could feel a manipulation of my body, working on the very bones of my back. Sometimes even a miracle seems to happen slowly, but the Spirit of the Lord was saying, "NOW!"

If we love someone—really love them—we don't disappoint them. And God never disappoints us. Through the pain I felt the room filled with the Presence, the Presence of

Love. The experience is beyond description! It was a deep soul experience, but at the moment I knew what was happening. "This is my healing!"

"I am experiencing the redemptive love of God!"

Through the power and the love of Jesus Christ, our Mediator, His love was NOW made real in my life. In this realization I fell asleep to awaken in the morning completely free of pain.

This experience took place some four years ago and there has been no recurrence of pain, even in a small degree. I have complete freedom of movement. The Lord has proven to me that He is always with me. I have found a peace within that bears witness to "The Light."

Our Lord once said: "YE ARE THE LIGHT OF THE WORLD. A CITY THAT IS SET ON A HILL CANNOT BE HID." (Matt. 5:14) Many people who are not aware of this healing experience have said to me, "Kay, there is something different about you." I agree that I have changed for the better and give thanks that my healing was of the soul·as well as of the body.

MEDITATION

Liberation From the Past

Dear Lord,

I, too, have been bound to past mistakes and fears and griefs. Now I come in quiet confidence and give them all to You. Take them from me, Lord. Cleanse me mentally and emotionally. Set me free and heal my soul.

Help my mind and body to respond and report on Your peace and harmony. I accept my freedom now because I feel it is Your gracious will that I be strong. I trust Your will,

57

and I am free now to concentrate on the things to be done by me this day.

The past is gone, even as the water that flows under the bridge. I could not bring it back even if I tried. Today needs my full attention. I accept Your freeing love, dear Lord.

Thank You, Jesus.

Amen.

CHAPTER 15

DISGUISED AS A STRANGER

THEN SHALL THE KINGDOM OF HEAVEN BE LIKENED UNTO TEN VIRGINS, WHICH WENT FORTH TO MEET THE BRIDEGROOM. AND FIVE OF THEM WERE WISE, AND FIVE WERE FOOLISH . . . AND THE FOOLISH SAID UNTO THE WISE, GIVE US OF YOUR OIL; FOR OUR LAMPS ARE GONE OUT. BUT THE WISE ANSWERED SAYING, NOT SO . . . GO . . . BUY FOR YOURSELVES. AND WHILE THEY WENT TO BUY, THE BRIDEGROOM CAME; AND THEY THAT WERE READY WENT IN WITH HIM TO THE MARRIAGE; AND THE DOOR WAS SHUT . . . WATCH THEREFORE, FOR YE KNOW NEITHER THE DAY NOR THE HOUR WHEREIN THE SON OF MAN COMETH.

—Matthew 25:1–13

I was one of many Christians who never read the Bible and therefore did not remember or never knew that Jesus promised to send His Spirit in the form of the Holy Comforter to guide, instruct, and unite man with God by resurrecting him. I contented myself by attending church occasionally, contributing to charity yearly, and conforming to the ways of the world. In other words, I was a dead Christian. I had not allowed the Holy Comforter to activate God's Holy Spirit in my life and affairs.

When a friend reported an incident that had happened to her recently, I was jolted into a new realization of what Christianity is all about. How could I have subjected myself to Church all these years and never understood the message before?

By evidence unquestionable, the Holy Comforter is present in the world today and not only prepares us for resurrection in Jesus Christ through Holy Communion, but guides, heals, and instructs us, even as Jesus said He would.

As we read the Bible, we are helped to understand how this can happen and that it certainly has happened before. In the seventh Chapter of the Gospel of John it explains that "the Holy Comforter was not yet given; because Jesus was not yet glorified." Then in the sixteenth Chapter, verse seven, Jesus told His followers, "It is expedient for you that I go away: for if I go not away, the Comforter will not come unto you; but if I depart, I will send him unto you."

Jesus, as a human person, could only be present physically in one place at one time, but His Spirit, the universal Person of the Holy Comforter, can be all places at once. He is God with us. This is a marvelous thing to realize!

This also explains the reason for miracle healers, and the Charismatic movement. In these latter days the Holy Comforter is very active, stirring God's Holy Spirit within the soul of man. Through His action people are being resurrected into a new awareness of what life is all about. We are not born just to die and go to heaven. There is more to it. We are to become resurrected beings with Jesus Christ! This requires diligent activity within the Spirit and through the guidance of Jesus Christ, our Saviour. He meets each one of us on our level of need and elevates us to His glorious estate.

In the twenty-fourth Chapter of Luke we read of two men who were walking on the road to Emmaus. Cleopas was one of the two. They evidently were talking about the crucifixion and resurrection of Jesus and were puzzled, searching for the reason for it all. Our Bible tells us that Jesus appeared in human form as a stranger. He entered into conversation with them and explained to them the reason for Jesus' crucifixion and resurrection and referred to ancient prophecy concerning His tremendous act of grace in our behalf.

The record goes on to say, our Lord "took bread, and blessed it, and brake, and gave to them. And their eyes were opened, and they knew Him. . . . and He vanished out of their sight."

In Acts 9:4 the Apostle Paul told the people about the Spirit of Jesus Christ appearing to him *after* His crucifixion, resurrection, and ascension, and speaking to him on the road to Damascus.

These are only a few of several cases recorded in the Bible that tell us how the Holy Comforter became immediately active. He has been working all these years with individuals and is especially active today.

This is the incident reported by my friend. She and her boy friend were driving along on a beautiful Sunday afternoon enjoying the fall foliage. He owned a small, two-door car, so when they stopped to pick up a bearded hitch-hiker dressed in white robes my friend had to open her door, lean forward and allow the hitch-hiker to get into the back seat.

As the car picked up speed again, the stranger entered into conversation with them about religion. Eventually he asked if either of them had attended church that day. They replied that they hadn't.

There was a pause and then the hitch-hiker asked: "Do you really believe in Jesus Christ?"

Surprised at this rather odd conversation, the driver of the car looked around and asked, "Why do you ask?"

To his utter amazement there was no one on the back

seat. The stranger had completely vanished. All that remained as evidence was the buckled seat belt and their memory of a brief conversation. The stranger could not possibly have gotten out except one of them move aside to open the door, and the car had been traveling at high speed. The autumn weather was cool, so the windows were closed.

The amazed couple were shocked and frightened. What could have happened? Who could it have been? Where did He vanish to? What should they do? These and many other questions flooded their thoughts.

After discussing it at length they decided that since it was such an unusual experience they should stop at the next town, swing off the turnpike, and report it. This they did. After finding the police station and telling their experience, they asked the desk sergeant, "Don't you think this is an unusual experience?"

"It is slightly irregular," he admitted, "especially since this is the sixth report of its kind today."

MEDITATION

Preparedness

Dear Lord,

You have many disguises, and I should be ready to see You at any moment. There have been times when I would have gladly invited You in, but other times I would have been very embarrassed to have had You walk in on me!

Now, I know You are invisibly present. You have known and seen everything concerning me thus far. Believe me, I am going to see to it that I remember this! I want to be in a position of suddenly remembering, "Jesus Christ is here," and being glad You *are* here! Maybe You will show Your blessed Self to me some day.

I liked Your story about the ten virgins, Lord. The five that were foolish had no oil in their lamps. This means they were not prepared to have You around. The five wise virgins had their lamps lit and went in with You to the feast. I intend to be like the five wise ones.

Believe me, Lord, I'm glad for Your warning and I will be prepared daily to please You in every way! Thank You, Lord.

Amen.

CHAPTER 16

PRAY!

I SAW IN THE NIGHT VISIONS, AND, BEHOLD, ONE
LIKE THE SON OF MAN CAME WITH THE CLOUDS OF
HEAVEN. . . . HIS DOMINION IS AN EVERLASTING
DOMINION, WHICH SHALL NOT PASS AWAY, AND
HIS KINGDOM THAT WHICH SHALL NOT BE
DESTROYED.

—Daniel 7:13,14

In the past I have dismissed dreams as fantasy, but recently I have read various articles and books on the subject. I now realize that most dreams have significance and that some dreams can have profound meaning. This is especially true of the type of dream that might be called a night vision. The Bible has many references to such. It is apparent that this is one means God has of speaking to us through our subconscious phase of mind.

In searching the Scripture for specific verification of this, I found that most of the great prophets and leaders of our race were guided by God from time to time in this way. Because of this, they derived extra determination and fortitude to bring forth more of God's goodness into man's experience.

There is the record in Genesis 31:11 of where Jacob told Rachel, "The angel of God spoke unto me in a dream, saying, Jacob: and I said, Here am I." The text continues with the exciting adventure he had because of this leading. Joseph dreamed many dreams of prophecy, all of which came to pass.

It was through a dream that Gideon was inspired by God to defeat the Midianites. The great Hebrew visionary, Daniel, dreamed many visions to which Jesus referred. Regarding this, we recall how the child Jesus' life was preserved when his earthly father, Joseph, was "warned of God in a dream to take the young child and his mother, and flee into Egypt and be there until I bring thee word." This is found in Matthew 2:13.

I found listed in my Bible Concordance many other interesting visions that have been given to man while in the dreaming state.

My dream was not of such consequence as the one I have mentioned, but it was very meaningful to me. It seemed that I was on an island. It was off the coast and could be reached by crossing the breakwater at low tide. There was just one old, weather-beaten house on this beautiful island with its lovely beaches. It was a particularly nice day. The sky was a vivid blue with large white, billowy clouds floating leisurely above. I sat down to rest and watch the swallows joyously swooping in large circles above my head.

They were so beautiful and colorful. They seemed to be so thrilled to be alive in such beautiful surroundings.

The swallows began to playfully dart here and there and then to my amazement the figure of Jesus appeared to be coming out of a beautiful white cloud. His arms were outstretched as He came toward me. The majesty of His presence was overpowering!

Then, as the playful swallows started flying around in large circles, they formed a picture of the open Bible. It was a very impressive sight with each tiny bird holding its place in the formation. Across the pages of the open Bible appeared one word—a very important word for me and for all the world. The word was *PRAY*!

This was His message to me. I was to pray as I had never prayed before. It was imperative that I pray—pray for myself, my friends and loved ones, and for the world! The world needs our prayers. It needs a lot of prayers to bring it back to God.

After I had received a deep impression of the seriousness of this message, Christ faded from view and the swallows dispersed. I awoke and realized that God, indeed, had been talking to me. Me, an ordinary office worker! But then I remembered that God is no respecter of persons. He loves us all equally well. This is especially true when we do His will. What a joy it is to follow and obey!

MEDITATION

Prayer

Dear Lord,

So You want me to pray? This is the first time I have tried to talk to You. I guess I'm kind of clumsy so forgive me. You feel so close and intimate I feel as though You are my best Friend. I guess this is so. You are my Teacher, my Guide also. You are my Saviour and I love You, Lord.

Now that I have said this, what shall I say? Do You really want to know what's on my mind? I guess You know anyway, but You want me to talk it out with You and listen to Your counsel. You have good reasons, no doubt.

If my words have some way of blessing someone else, I'll gladly cooperate. Perhaps You need my help here. Well, here I am. And I am going to talk about myself and my problems first. And when I finish, I'll listen. And then I'll pray for the rest of the good folks in the world. O.K? First about me, and then the world. And then I am going to listen a long while so You can correct me and teach me how to pray better. . . .

Amen.

CHAPTER 17

FAR FROM HOME—BUT SAFE

ASK, AND IT SHALL BE GIVEN YOU: SEEK, AND YE
SHALL FIND: KNOCK, AND IT SHALL BE OPENED
UNTO YOU.

—Luke 11:9

I feel an infilling of the Holy Spirit as I share this account
of a strange and inspiring journey. It was on this trip that
my family and I met God in a never-to-be-forgotten crisis.
At that time we came to know the Glorious Presence.

My husband had summers off from work and because of
this our family usually did a good deal of traveling. This
particular summer of which I write we had decided to swap
our eastern home with a family on the west coast. On our
way west we thought it would be nice to visit Yellowstone
National Park. We had always wanted to see it and this
seemed to be the ideal opportunity.

We arrived at Yellowstone, rented a cabin and settled
down to enjoy a week of hiking, fishing and geyser viewing.
There seemed to be a variety of interesting activities and we
were eager to participate.

The next day, however, our older daughter did not feel
very well. She offered to rest in bed while we went out in
the hot sun. We, believing it to be just a spell of temporary
fatigue, prayed with her and let her stay in bed while we
went off in a boat to fish.

When we returned and showed her a large lake trout, she did not respond with any enthusiasm, nor was she interested in the next day's plans. In fact, she was still in bed.

The following day she appeared worse. Actually she was so ill she could not sit up without being propped and she couldn't eat. "Hold up your head, honey," we prompted. But she couldn't. She seemed painfully ill and especially weak in her spine.

Becoming alarmed, we prayed the more earnestly. In the past whenever anything had happened to our children we had asked in prayer, believing that God would heal it, and He always did. But this sickness appeared different—and we were far from home.

We continued to pray and to know that she was a child of God and that God was her all-loving, all-powerful Father and also the only true substance, life, and health of her mind and body. We rehearsed how He loved her and that God was present with her. We knew He was capable and willing to heal her. No change appeared evident and we wondered if our prayers helped her. I am sure everyone sooner or later meets this same question. In spite of our prayers she appeared on the verge of collapse.

Since we were miles from any doctor or hospital that we knew of, we decided to drive for Salt Lake City, Utah, as fast as we could get her there. By taking turns driving, my husband and I covered the distance, hardly stopping. We arrived at a hospital outpatient department about five minutes before the staff doctors were to leave for the day.

I recall, a kind, Chinese doctor and several other doctors stayed after hours and took many samples. They all examined our daughter thoughtfully and then decided to administer a very large dose of penicillin.

"You have a very sick child," we were told. "Bring her

back tomorrow and we will make a bed for her somehow."
The hospital was full to overflowing. They expressed grave
concern again and told us it appeared to be spinal meningitis. We didn't know then, but we were not to return to
the hospital again. We did know, though, that God never
made anything like spinal meningitis and since it was man
made, it had no real power over our child. So we denied it!

At the same time we also saw the toll this false sickness
was taking from our child. We were discouraged that our
prayers and Truth-knowing had not brought freeing results.
What more were we supposed to do? We asked for divine
guidance.

The beautiful words of a hymn came to mind, "If with
all your heart ye truly seek me, ye shall surely find me."
We held on to God and full faith, knowing that somehow
He was our answer. He would either heal her or tell us to
take our child back again to the hospital and help her there.
We knew God used human hands and human ways often
to bless His children, but we asked for and wanted a divine
healing for her.

We had another pressing problem, too. Where could we
stay? The city was full to overflowing. Every motel or tourist
house had signs up: "NO VACANCY." We mustered the
faith to know God had a right place for us to stay and He
would take care of us all.

After praying in the car, we were guided to drive out onto
the hillside overlooking the city. There in front of us was
another motel with another "NO VACANCY" sign lighted
up in red.

We did not lose heart. God was with us and He would
provide! Just as we drew near, a car was checking out. We
drove in and the owner allowed us to move in immediately.
The linen had been stripped from the room and bath, and

70

the beds needed to be made up, but at least we had a roof over our heads.

As soon as we got inside, our daughter slid to the floor and started to hemorrhage. We prayed fervently, "GOD HELP US!" Immediately, the Lord stopped the flow of blood. The Lord also provided miraculously a cloth for us to bathe our child and clean the floor so that the manager did not see it when he returned shortly with the clean linen. He observed our child was ill, however, and the next morning instead of asking us to leave, he kindly offered us a little white house, quietly apart from the motel, which we gratefully accepted. I have often blessed him for this kindness.

The next morning we continued to pray, comfort and care for our child. We read the Bible while our little girl lay hot in bed. We wanted so much for God's perfection to shine forth in complete healing. But we did not want to jeopardize her health, either, by denying her hospital help if this was what was needed. We knew that healing of our child depended a good deal upon the consciousness of the parents. So we tried valiantly to remain faith-filled and confident in God despite the discouraging outer picture.

We struggled with the decision. Finally my husband and I dressed and prepared to take her back to the hospital. We were reluctant and she cried and said she didn't want to go. We felt awful. It was a terrible decision to have to make.

As my husband and I stood in the hallway for one final prayer before carrying her to the car to take her back to the hospital, a strange and wonderful thing happened. While our heads were bowed, the presence of our Lord, Jesus Christ, entered our midst. We both felt Him join us and we both sensed His coming at the same time.

He stood there with us and we felt His great power and

authority. We sensed Him taking command of the situation. A deep, overwhelming joy swept over us. We looked jubilantly at each other with tears streaming down our faces. All was well! Our daughter was healed. We just KNEW this as surely as we knew her name.

Praise God! Our prayers had been answered. Oh, how grateful we were to know we had a Saviour who cares! We had a Personal God who had come to help us—to comfort and to heal! I have no words to express what we felt in those precious moments when we became aware of the Glorious Presence.

At the same time our daughter called out to us, "Oh, Mommy—Daddy! I am going to be all right! I KNOW it. Jesus just told me!"

It was so beautiful, I can't describe it. Praise welled up and thanksgiving swept over us all. We clung together, laughing, crying and praising God. We thought of the man in the temple whom Jesus healed and who went "walking, and leaping, and praising God!" (Acts 3:8) This is what we felt like doing with our daughter.

We may have been far from home, but we certainly were not far from God! We had an unfailing Friend traveling with us. Within three days our child was so well no trace of illness remained. We journeyed on to California without delay.

In California we settled into the house we had been given for the summer. The next day we went to the airport and met friends who had previously arranged to visit us for a couple of weeks. Our daughter was so perfectly well and happy they never dreamed she had been sick the week before and we never mentioned it.

Our little girl had a wonderful, active summer—free from even a cold, and she has been perfectly well these past twenty-five years.

We have come to believe that there may be times when the negative race thought attacks people so viciously that it is only by denying it and asking for the additional help and grace of the Glorious Presence of Jesus Christ that it can be overcome. He overcame the world, so when we unite with Him, success is guaranteed. We need Him. He knew that we would need Him and that must be part of the reason why He promised to return and be with us. World problems are not lessening and He is needed now even more than before.

We are grateful that our Lord taught us this valuable lesson in Person. Not everyone has yet been so blessed. I am convinced, though, that it is only a matter of time when every soul in the world that is receptive to God will know Him on a personal basis.

We of ourselves can turn Godward at any time. Humble, sincere prayer is the safest, truest and fastest route to God awareness. "It is the Father within that doeth the works," even as Jesus said. "I am the Way" unto the Father. So, we praise and give thanks for the mediating power, love and grace of our Lord, Jesus Christ, who brings miracles and blessings to us.

MEDITATION

Ask

Dear Lord,

Why is it that we worldlings think we are so self-sufficient? Why do we put off asking for Your help? You have told us over and over again to simply ASK. That is simple.

I have a problem, dear Lord. I now ask Your help in this healing need. I know Your power is sufficient to right any situation whether it appears big or small to me. You have the perfect sight that clears away all false appearance and brings health and wholeness. You know only perfection.

Heal my soul first, dear Lord, I ask. Help me to conform to Your orderly process of thought and action. Help me to release myself to God. Help me to know the power that runs the universe is sufficient to bind up all my wounds, cleanse me from self-imposed limitations, and heal my bad habits.

Help me to cast all doubt or fear from my thought. Guide me into the realization of peaceful assurance that You CAN and *will* answer. Thank You, Lord.

Amen.

CHAPTER 18

RECOGNIZING CHRIST JESUS

THE LORD IS MY LIGHT AND MY SALVATION:
WHOM SHALL I FEAR?

—Psalm 27:1

I was seventeen years old, uncertain of what I was capable of doing in life, puzzled as to why I was here, and not at all sure that Jesus Christ was real or that prayer was effective. In fact, experience seemed to prove that prayer did not "work," and I was meeting more and more people who, if the subject came up, expressed the opinion that Jesus was probably the best man who ever lived, but no more than that, and that no one could really prove anything about God.

One hot summer day I went for a walk alone, and when I came to the park, sat down on a bench in a quiet place to rest and enjoy the beauty of grass and trees and flowers and white-clouded sky. Suddenly, I noticed a growing radiance of light which seemed to suffuse me and everything else. It was unlike anything that had ever happened to me before, and as I waited breathless and attentive, a great peace stole over me.

Somehow I received the assurance that my desire to be a singer could be fulfilled (in spite of the fact that I had up to now been too shy even to speak before people), if I would do my part. Eventually the light faded, but the feeling of ultimate victory remained and saw me through many a struggle.

I had never desired to make money from singing or even to have a career—only to be able to do well the thing I enjoyed most—and that is the way, of course, that it turned out. I took part in choral groups, sang in church choirs, was a soloist, and even had opportunities to perform in an amateur opera company.

While I had no vision of Jesus Christ and heard no voice then, it seemed as if Jesus must have been the light. I did not share this experience until recently, feeling that it was something sacred between Him and me, too precious to risk being lost by exposure to the influence of someone's possible disbelief or even ridicule. And so, like Mary, I "pondered these things in my heart" until they came to pass.

A number of times I have heard my name called, usually when I was in a deep sleep. I would automatically sit up in bed and answer, only to find no one there. Often it was a man's voice, which I interpreted as Jesus', and I would wonder what He wanted to tell me or have me do. But there have been no further words at such times. However, it did focus my attention more often and deeply on the unseen side of life, prompting me to search in books and lectures for more understanding. Once, or perhaps twice, the voice was that of a woman, and that also was puzzling. Was it Mary's voice? Was it a guardian angel speaking? It did not sound like anyone I knew.

Years later, when I married, we went to live in Denver. Shortly afterward I began to have dizzy spells which my husband assured me were due to the change in altitude, and I would soon get adjusted and be all right. By this time I had had some metaphysical study and was using denial and affirmation.

But one day while I was shopping in a department store I was overtaken by a peculiar weakness and vertigo so that I had to hold on to a counter to keep from falling. Someone noticed and brought a chair. People are so kind! A little group gathered and a concerned lady offered to take me home, but after a few moments of rest and inward prayer I was able to get up and go home alone. I did not mention the incident and felt good all evening. My husband had to go to work early the next morning so he said he would get breakfast on the way. When I awoke I sat on the edge of the bed a moment, violently dizzy again. I denied its power and asked God's help. Instantly a movement like an electric shock went through my head, and a man's voice said, "You don't have to be sick!" Immediately the disturbance vanished and has never returned.

Again years passed, and we went back to my home to care for my parents, who needed our help. The third year we were with them, my mother was in the hospital, very ill. I took time out to go to church one Sunday, and during the sermon as I sat in the choir loft, my gaze was upon a favorite stained glass window, a beautiful portrait of Jesus as the Good Shepherd carrying a lamb in His arm. I was thinking of my mother being held like the lamb, and comforted by His staff. Once again, as before, the atmosphere changed. I could hear the speaker, occasional coughs and rustlings, yet everything was charged with an electrified calmness. Light was everywhere. How was it different than usual? I could not tell, yet it was *there* with eyes opened *or closed.* I glanced about to see whether any of the choir members were aware of something different, but none seemed to be. So I sat and blissfully absorbed it until time for our next choir response, when things returned to "normal."

Or was it normal? Through these and other experiences,

I have come to believe that the return is to the *ab*normal. We have accepted and are having to work our way through this earthplane experience back to our normal, which is our original consciousness of the kingdom of heaven. Jesus brought this kingdom of heaven consciousness to earth, and we too must bring it into manifestation here and now. It is our privilege and destiny to help Him develop ourselves and all the earth into a new dimension of life. But first we have to recognize it inwardly as Jesus Christ gets through to us in some way. Then we must practice and live it until all is fulfilled.

MEDITATION

Awareness

Dear Lord,

How easy it is to become wrapped up in worldly aspirations. And how generously You answer our requests. You seem to know we need to have the experiences we desire, even though it is not the ultimate aim of our souls. How patiently You bear with us along the highway of our explorations, and how kindly You deal with our faults and short-comings.

I would be aware of Your presence, Lord. You have told us the kingdom of heaven is here. Help me to behold its radiance even as You did for the woman in this story.

I believe heaven is here, Lord. I know this is where You have Your abode. Open my eyes that I may see—open my ears that I may hear—and open my awareness so that Your glorious heaven may become a reality to me. Thank You, Lord.

Amen.

CHAPTER 19

BLUE EYES

HIS EYES ARE UPON THE WAYS OF MAN, AND HE
SEETH ALL HIS GOINGS.

—Job 34:21

You know how it is when you are growing up. You think
life is great and you want to live it all at once! I could
hardly wait to get to be sixteen so I could step out on my
own. At last I turned sixteen and my father gave me a
second-hand Plymouth car. It was blue and had real neat
lines. But my happiness was brief.

I received the car at twelve noon and at twelve midnight
that same day I met with a terrible accident. The car was
such a total wreck it could not even be towed away. It had
to be picked up in a heap and carried to the dump.

I was rushed to the hospital unconscious where it was
found among other things that I had a fractured vertebra
in my upper spine. I was placed in a cast and then in a
brace, which I took off after about a year. As a result of
my spinal problem my whole body was thrown off balance.
This caused the bones at the neck end of my spine to stick
out awkwardly and my whole back bent painfully forward.

In the mornings my feet felt dead. I was told to expect
these conditions to become increasingly worse with time and
that there was no hope for my condition to ever improve.
I was too young and too uninformed to think healing was
even possible.

In fact, I was much more concerned for a friend than for myself. This friend was also suffering as the result of an accident. Her pain was intensive due to the fact that there was no cartilage in her hip socket and the hip bones were like lace-work. My concern for her was so strong that I began to consider ways and means of other possible healing since the doctors could offer no help for either of us.

About this time the Cayce philosophy came to our attention. We studied it along with our Bibles and were led to realize the possibility of Christ healing us by prayer. This belief really took hold of both of us and our faith increased. We also considered other various possibilities for healing. This all took place just before I had a series of very strange ''dreams'' and was liberated from my physical distress.

I will list the ''dreams'' as ''Dreams One, Two, and Three'' and tell you about them so you can praise the Lord with me for His goodness. You can see as you read my account that Christ certainly uses unique ways to reach and heal people!

DREAM ONE: I seemed to be in a certain doctor's office, awaiting my operation. It was a dark room, thronged with many low quality people of unreliable character it seemed to me. It was obvious, though, that regardless of their character they expected the doctor to help them. I was impressed that I should be watchful of myself and stay on the straight and narrow path with Christ Jesus, as only in that way could I ever expect to be healed.

I felt quite unsure of myself in this company. I also wondered if this would be just another disappointment. Perhaps the doctor had forgotten me. I wondered if he remembered my appointment or anything about me.

Then I heard my name called. The doctor came in. When I turned to look at Him I was in the presence of a man with terrifically magnetizing, piercing blue eyes. I have never in my life seen such eyes. As His eyes looked into mine I felt a strong current of God's great power stream from Him into me. It was a wonderful feeling. I knew that He had not forgotten my appointment and to my surprise He did remember my name. To my amazement He knew my case intimately.

The dream convinced me that the "doctor" was definitely "on the job" in my behalf; he had divine power sufficient for any challenge and he was willing to use his power to heal me. With that, the "dream" ended.

This first "dream" served much as an introduction, preparing my thought to receive my healing. Readiness is an important factor in any case. It teaches us that what seems impossible to man is possible to God.

DREAM TWO: It seemed that I was going home. I was first in an airport, but after some confusion of missing my flight I found myself many miles away in a small country town. It seemed friendly and comfortable. I entered an old pharmacy and found it to be a store with great charm. I was impressed with its old-fashioned quality, with herb drawers, white porcelain jars, mortar and pestle and other means for natural help.

Soon the pharmacist walked in from the back room and came up to me. I felt his eyes upon me and looked up into his very soft blue eyes. But suddenly I felt the same overwhelming power penetrating into me from this man that I had previously felt in the eyes of the doctor. Somehow, the same Spirit of Christ was present, although outwardly disguised in a different way. The original feeling of great power poured into my soul. Then in addition to this I felt a tremendous stirring of great love.

His love enveloped me completely. It was so overpowering I collapsed into a chair and cried and cried. He knelt and compassionately embraced me.

Never have I felt such recognition of the inner me. It was as though He knew the very deepest part of me. His love reached into the core of my being and I sensed the glory of the risen Christ.

The two dreams then became as one with power and love united, with me as the full object of His devotion. With this I awoke.

DREAM THREE: I returned to the first waiting room and once again came into the presence of the doctor with the powerful, healing blue eyes who, I knew this time, loved me. My friend had received help and urged me to also, so I cooperated in every way. I was told to "reach up to the end of the table and pull to the South—to the South— the South." As I pulled, a great force began to fill me. It started at the base of my spine and began rising through the length of my back.

When it got to the damaged part of my spine it met with some resistance, but gradually it pushed through and straightened out my back. The manipulation was then over. I climbed down off the table and stood upright, taller and straighter than ever before. I felt very thrilled and excited and extremely grateful.

I pulled out my wallet to freely give all the money I had to this, my wonderful Friend, the Great Physician. But my friend convinced me that I should wait until later when I might have more to give Him.

With this I awoke. I was healed! I awoke my friends who gathered in the kitchen and looked me over. It was true. They confirmed my convictions. As they examined me they found a scar on my back that I had had for about fifteen years which was usually hardly noticeable. It was now a bright pink. The hair on my back was pushed in two different directions as carefully as though it had been parted with a comb.

The most noticeable results to me of this healing, besides an improvement in posture, was the fact that my feet no longer had the heavy dead feeling in the morning! This condition had bothered me for years, ever since the accident.

Also, the vertebra at the base of my neck that had caused stiff neck and headaches, had flattened out. From that day on, stiff necks and headaches vanished. I have been free ever since. A fourth dream instructed me to continue exercising, reaching up and "pulling South." I obeyed His instructions and continued feeling fine.

Soon after this series of strange "dreams" I returned to our local osteopath who had looked at me several times a few years before this—in fact, it was right after the accident.

He took X-rays and reported no noticeable change in the spinal structure, but he could see how well and tall I stood now. He was puzzled and could not verify it by scientific means. He kept remarking that the change in my posture was "most remarkable and unexplainable." He could offer no further explanation.

I had no doubt, nor did any of my friends, as to what had happened. Jesus Christ, in one of His unique ways of reaching all kinds of people, had healed me! Not only was I changed physically, but emotionally as well. My soul had been made whole.

MEDITATION

Versatility

Dear Lord,

It is Your Presence that makes the difference in healing, I know. When I call that Presence forth, healing takes place. It is not the health resort, the doctor, or the medication that heals. The rest are instruments of Yours. Without You, no one could be healed. You connect us to God-life, dear Lord, so that health is assured when we become one with You.

May I always remember Your versatility. May I be generous when others seem to be looking for You in a place I think You may not be. Help me to know that You have as many paths to healing as there are people in this world. You have a way of being just anywhere, and especially in the place that anyone might look!

Amen.

CHAPTER 20

A HUNTING EPISODE

THE EARNEST EXPECTATION OF THE CREATURE
WAITETH FOR THE MANIFESTATION OF THE SONS
OF GOD.

—Romans 8:19

All life is sacred because life is God's gift to man. There is a beautiful legend about a knight who once lived in France during the 6th Century. He had an unusual experience with the Lord through a hunting episode.

One day, as legend tells us—on Good Friday to be exact—he was hunting in the forest of Ardennes in northern France. He had his bow and arrows with him and hoped to take back some fresh venison for a festive party. He had not gone far when he came across a beautiful stag, peacefully grazing in a lovely woodland clearing by a brook.

Complimenting himself on his good fortune, St. Hubert raised his bow, preparing to shoot the stag. The stag raised his head and stood quietly looking at Hubert.

Suddenly, a heavenly light shone around the stately creature's head and a crucifix appeared on its forehead between its antlers. Out of the silence the Lord's voice admonished him for his careless attitude about the precious gift of life in all creatures both great and small.

The knight sank to his knees and humbly begged pardon. With deep remorse St. Hubert prayed: "O little stag, I see

thou hast the Lord, and if thou hast, all have. It pitieth me
to think how many times I have slain Christ.''

When he finished praying, the lovely stag had gone.
Hubert left the forest and when he reached home he re-
nounced his life of ease and gaiety and resolved to serve
the Lord from thenceforth.

His extraordinary fervor for serving appealed to the local
Bishop of Maestricht and soon he was ordained a priest
forever. Later when the Bishop passed on, St. Hubert was
chosen to become his successor.

With ardent devotion to his Saviour, Jesus Christ, he
spent the rest of his days bringing an awareness of Christ
to many pagans in the Ardennes area.

Strangely enough, after his death, hunters chose good
St. Hubert as their Patron Saint.

MEDITATION

Sanctity

Dear Lord,

Let me not be unduly concerned with the materialistic
side of life. Let me attend to that which needs doing, but
let me look within each leaf I rake, each weed I pull, each
animal that runs across my lawn, each person I meet, and
behold the Christ. Let me quietly say, "I behold the Christ
in you."

As I do this I will soon forget the differences or the old

Sanctity of all life

M. Russell

complaints. I will find the sanctity of all life everywhere about me. Each day will be a holy day and I will treat every occasion as a delightful adventure. I will accept each person with respect.

O Creator of this beautiful earth plane, let me love every bit of You I see, and let me see You in all. Thank You, dear Lord.

Amen.

CHAPTER 21

FOUR A.M. SURPRISE

IT WAS MEET THAT WE SHOULD MAKE MERRY AND
BE GLAD: FOR THIS THY BROTHER WAS DEAD AND IS
ALIVE AGAIN: AND WAS LOST, AND IS FOUND!
—Luke 15:32

Four o'clock in the morning was my life-style before I
grew to respect and truly love my Saviour, Jesus Christ.
When you truly love someone, you always want to do those
things pleasing to him. As a child I loved Jesus and felt
called to serve Him when I grew up. But as we grow up,
the world has a way of taking over. I was faced with having
to earn a living at an early age.

I worked at various odd jobs until I found work as a
waiter in one of the better restaurants in our city. After
several years of working for them I was given a Maître d'
position. Soon, however, false appetites began to set in.

Over-indulgence in food soon gave me a wide spread
around the middle. Other indulgences showed signs of
dissipation in my face. I had many girl friends, but I liked
one in particular. She, however, also had many boy friends
and this is the way my life was spent. I drifted and began
working only when I needed money. Matters got pretty
bad and then one early morning, it happened!

I was driving back to my apartment from an all-night
party. Well, it wasn't exactly a party. I had been with some

acquaintances all night. As I drove along I saw a fellow walking along by the side of the street. I slowed up and stopped.

The man walked up beside the car and I stared at him as he looked in at me. There was something different about this man. Whatever it was, I liked it. I couldn't decide what is was but I got the feeling he was o.k. He was looking for a ride. I told him where I was going and he said that was near where he was going, too, so he got in. He was sober and clean. Although I had on a new suit, I felt quite dirty in his presence.

As we drove along he opened up on the subject of religion. So we began talking. What did I think about Jesus, he wanted to know. Did I ever pray? How did I like the church? Why was I out driving at such an early hour? Did I believe in God?

Usually, if anyone had tried to ask me such personal questions I would have resented it and told him off. But there was something regal about this man, yet something secure and humble also that made me forget myself. I began to really level with him.

He seemed quite at ease. The more we talked, the more at ease I became. I couldn't help but like him. I was quite impressed with his goodness and wisdom. I honestly replied that I hadn't been to church in a long while, not since Sunday School days probably.

Did I believe in God? Of course, I did! But I took a deep breath and admitted that life as I now found it was not very satisfying. There was something missing. Just what it was, I didn't know.

For some strange reason I felt elated in the presence of this man. He obviously had some answers I didn't have. I wondered what they were.

After a while he asked to get out. I pulled up and he

thanked me for the ride. Then he stepped out on the sidewalk and vanished into thin air. I couldn't believe my eyes!

I started up from the curb and sped down the road, oblivious of other cars or possible excessive speeding. By now it was daylight and I glanced nervously at the seat beside me where the stranger had sat.

Suddenly it seemed as though the whole of heaven fell down right on top of my head! There, on the seat beside me, was blood—and the memory of a cross. I put my finger out and gingerly touched it. It was REAL blood!

I jammed on the brakes and came to a sudden halt. It seemed like a sword was piercing my soul, slicing up separate sections of my life and paring them off one by one until almost nothing was left. The Holy Spirit swept into my soul, and man met God. By the roadside, in a city not yet awake, I was filled with clean, new life and I was reborn in the Christ Spirit.

When I reached home I scrubbed off the blood. That was the end of life as I had known it. From then on things were different.

You may consider this to be a wild tale of fantasy, but the Bible says to judge the tree by its fruit. The fruit of my life these many years has been good. Since my Christhood I have tried to the best of my ability to live a clean, upright life—one that I can be proud to present to God when my time of final reckoning comes. I realize that reckoning comes daily, hourly as I try to live up to the Jesus Christ standard. However, there will be a time of final reckoning when everyone will be called to report to God. I have learned that He takes no excuses. It is either yes or no—there is no middle road.

When you discover that someone has an interest in your life and he is not a long way off, but right with you on the job every minute night and day, it helps you. If I am ever tempted, I turn to God and He sets me straight real fast.

I have lots of friends in this world who do the same thing, but they are not always available when I need to talk to them. But the Glorious Presence is always with me and He always has just the right solution for every problem at hand. When we live close to Jesus we don't need to have problems that linger. I am grateful I have learned how to relate to God and live a wholesome, fulfilling life.

MEDITATION

Purity

Dear Lord,

You have said, "Blessed are the pure in heart: for they shall see God!" It is difficult to stay pure these days, You know. With all the filthy pictures in magazines and advertisements on the screen and on television, how can a person stay pure except he live with You?

I am grateful You live with me, Lord. You help me know immediately when something is not good viewing. You help me just walk out or turn it off or avoid seeing or hearing about it.

I ask that You take away from me any foul pictures or any false feelings that don't belong to a child of God.

Keep my heart so filled with You and the good life, I don't have any interest in the rubbish. I love You, Lord. I choose Your companionship over everything else. I will remain true to You and acceptable to You. Help me to stay pure. Thank You, Lord.

Amen.

CHAPTER 22

THE MEANING OF ONENESS

I IN THEM AND THOU IN ME, THAT THEY MAY BE
MADE PERFECT IN ONE.

—John 17:23

A profound change came into my life two weeks ago. I
would like to tell you about it as best I can. A good place
to start might be who I am and where I come from. I was
born, raised and basically educated in County Kerry in
Ireland, in a Roman Catholic family. I am the oldest of
twelve children. That means that I was basically oriented to
a high degree of responsibility from a very early age. That
became a weight to contend with as the years wore on. There
was no time in my family for emotional closeness with
parents, and life was strict and rigid.

My home was on a farm which represented our family
livelihood and while we were not rich, we had no feeling of
poverty or want.

On a personal level, the God that we knew then was very
difficult for me to absorb and I did not do so well. I
alternated between a sort of awesome fear and a rationalized
conclusion that none of this made any sense.

The upshot of all my questioning was that my ability to
relate to the possibility of a Divine Being was very low. I
only conceded that, on the basis that anything is possible,
I would guide my life on the basis that I would not do or

say or impose anything on anyone that I would not do to myself and that I would conduct my life as best I could towards an orientation that said, should there indeed be something beyond this life, then I want to be as far ahead in development, enlightenment or whatever else there is, as I possibly can be. I felt that the direction for this lay in reading, acquiring information and becoming indeed very learned.

I was married in England to an indifferent Catholic who was an alcoholic. For the survival of our children and for their material well-being, and to hold them together and maintain my home, I eventually divorced him.

My life has not been easy. I learned the meaning of insecurity and fear for survival when I came to Canada in 1953. It took me a long time to learn to cope with that. I came to a belief that seeking help in the Spirit was not going to rectify my state of affairs. Eventually when my children told me the only reason they were going to church on Sundays was to please me, I gave up. I had no good reason myself for doing this.

In 1973 I had to face the certainty that my family was my total responsibility. I went to school and took a twenty-credit program in business administration. It was a hard grind and a long haul. It took my total concentration because I don't really like that sort of thing, even though I can be quite effective at it.

Before that, I was involved in meeting all urgent demands for financial support of my family through creative means. I used sewing, crochet, macramé, demonstration classes, adult education activities—many, many ways. I was a good quality entrepreneur, moving mostly on my wits and motivated by fear, worry, anxiety and all the emotions and drives oriented to survival.

I learned to become strong, to stand up and be counted, to protect and work for what I believed in, and I believed firmly that if I could not count on myself, I could count on nothing or on nobody. It was a lonely way to go.

At the end of the business course, I was employed by the college where I now work, in the Theater Production department. I taught costume production. I had become good enough and skillful enough and convincing enough to take on the job. The business people thought I was foolish to take their courses and then turn around and teach costume making. However, I was trying to maintain a measure of autonomy, and some right to decide for myself and still do what I would prefer, rather than what I knew I had to do.

Eventually I moved into the administration staff and for a while carried both the office job and the teaching job. In the summer of 1975 I decided that I would go to the University and see what I could do there. I had a special reason for doing that and it was not really academic.

That winter I became involved in a relaxation and self-awareness program in an effort to combat stress that was causing me migraine headaches which lasted at least 80% of the average month. I felt that my life had all been lived for nothing in spite of my four rather lovely children, and I felt a total failure.

In March of that year I went through some rather odd experiences which frightened me. In trying to complete an assignment, one day I found myself writing with lightning speed and producing material that I had no reason to believe I had incorporated into my frame of knowledge. Somebody who read it said it was "pure metaphysics." I did not know what metaphysics was at the time. I found I could do this and tune into this sort of creative streak and make it work for me. I went to the University and put myself in a pressure situation where I had to do a lot of work just to test it.

There were also things like vivid visions, the ability to tune in to situations, and other variations that concerned me. I began to read everything I could on the abnormal or paranormal. I forced myself through psychology, psychiatry, medicine to some extent, research on altered states of consciousness and everything along this line I could find.

In these last three years, I have used very extensively the techniques of relaxation and stress reduction that I used and learned along the way, along with a full-time job. I have managed to almost complete a degree in Adult Education. I have given several lectures and I seemed to have a good relationship with my children based on talking to one another, mutual trust and respect for one another. All the time, I felt very positive about what I had achieved and managed to do and become. I felt that I could carry it on as long as I could depend on myself. I never permitted myself to think that would stop.

But at the back of my mind that nagging fear was always there—"what if anything happens to me?" I just did not permit myself to consider it and pressed on as hard and as best as I could.

This brings me to about a month ago. I was almost at the end of my semester. It was the last Wednesday in March and I had missed three classes because I had been ill and I was very tired. I was prepared to miss that night, too, but a fellow student called and said we should go. Someone was substituting for our professor that night and before I went home I had almost decided that I would attend his course, Creative Awareness, which was starting the following week.

I got acute bronchitis the following week, but for some reason I went anyway. As the priest gave his lectures over the week and treated the Bible, the story of Jesus and of Moses, and other aspects he covers, I thought, "This almost makes sense. Maybe I should look at it. It would be nice to be able to relate to this." A more unspiritual approach, a less committed or unemotional response would be hard to define. I was just prepared to consider it.

It also happened that, during the previous few weeks, there had been a particular family problem which had been there for some time, that was really a nagging worry to me. On the last occasion the problem happened, I gave a brief thought to the possibility that there might be a God out there somewhere.

I asked, if there were, would He please help me. It was not a loud appeal, nor a convinced one. I was just pretty desperate.

One Sunday of the course I have just talked about, there was a long lunch hour from the lectures. The instructor celebrated Mass. I had not been to Mass for twelve years except for the two funeral Masses for my parents. I had no emotional attachment to the situation whatsoever. I took a look at the prayer book and was glad I would be able to follow it, in a casual sort of way. It did not occur to me that the day would be any different from any other day.

While we were waiting for the Mass to begin, as I sat there alone, I closed my eyes and allowed myself to relax.

I did not remember later what happened. All that stood out was the opening statement of the priest in a loud, ringing voice, "CHRIST IS RISEN!" At that moment I was aware of a blinding impact and I found myself displaced. I seemed to be out of the country. There was a large rock background in this lonesome place, but I knew the person standing there in His flowing white robe was indeed Christ.

In a mighty impact, over a split second, I just knew, Christ is Risen! It was not right close up, but I was there and He was there and I simply knew. He was looking at me and He was with me and He was part of me.

It was all just too much and the tears were pouring down my cheeks. I had a quick thought that I would have to stop, that I would have to wipe them, but I didn't. It really wasn't that important. What mattered was the overwhelming realization that God was really there, that Jesus was

97

really with us, and that He is reachable and available and that one can actually talk to Him. It was just too much for me in that moment of time.

Shortly after that first moment of impact, the priest led the congregation in the hymn, "Put your hand in His nail-scarred hand," and He was there beside me. The tears were still flowing and I could not cope with seeing His face. I didn't feel bad—I just was so overwhelmed, so tremendously overawed and at the same time, so very grateful, so confused, and so joyous all at the same time, that I did not know what to do.

As the words were repeated, "Put your hand in His nail-scarred hand," the hand and the arm with the white sleeve was there before me. I did not look further; I just gave myself up to the peace and joy of the realization that there was after all a Source, a place of solace, a refuge! Without realizing what was happening, I had in that second acquired not only a realization of the reality of Jesus, but also of the reality of my own soul.

Then and there, in that hotel room as the Mass proceeded, I put my hand in His hand and my life has not been the same again, nor will it ever be.

Shortly after that experience I became almost frantic because I could find no way to "repay" the debt I owed the Lord for His great gift of grace I had received just one week before.

The problem was that never before had I been given something of any magnitude, or even something little, without some strings attached. I wanted to pay my debt! Because I was so upset, one night I decided that I would hand over the problem to God, go to sleep, and expect an answer in the morning. As I became awake, this thought came to me, "THE LORD DOES NOT DEAL IN TRADE-OFFS."

I suddenly became aware that I had not been asked to pay anything! I had been given a great gift and I was not dealing with someone who was in the habit of making trades. His love is not to be bought; it goes beyond price. There was no cost. I could accept it and be happy or I could reject it. It was all up to me. I did not have an obligation to pay a debt. I was my own problem!

The lesson I learned at that moment was that there is a time for everything and the Lord will have me do what *He* wants, not what *I* think He wants or what I think would be a good thing to do.

In the days that have passed, my life has been a discovery of inner strength and capacity that was His all along, only I didn't know it.

MEDITATION

Oneness

Dear Lord,

You are the risen Christ! You have overcome the world and all the temptations of error. You are with me and a part of me and I am glad, glad, glad! Your body is so sweet; Your blood is so rich. It flows in my veins and I am Yours.

Oh, Lord, this ecstasy is so beautiful.

I know our oneness, that sweet, sure bond of peace. A peace no one and no thing can ever take from me. You paid my price, O precious Saviour. No longer must I struggle alone. You bought me with Your pure blood and I am wholly Yours.

Thank You for sharing Yourself with me. We are one!

Amen.

CHAPTER 23

HUMBLE YOURSELF AS A LITTLE CHILD

WHOSOEVER THEREFORE SHALL HUMBLE HIMSELF
AS THIS LITTLE CHILD, THE SAME IS GREATEST IN
THE KINGDOM OF HEAVEN. AND WHOSO SHALL
RECEIVE ONE SUCH LITTLE CHILD IN MY NAME
RECEIVETH ME.

—Matthew 18:4,5

What would you do if you met Jesus? This question was
asked of me when I was a very little girl. After thinking
a moment I blurted, "Why, I would shake His hand!"
After this, I would say to myself, "When I meet Jesus I
will shake His hand." This continued until an unusual
thing happened to me when I was about ten years old.

One frosty winter's evening after being tucked into bed,
I drifted off into dreamland as usual. Little did I realize
that tonight my dream would come true!

Suddenly I found myself walking in an emerald-green
field. The grass was as soft as a new carpet. I happened
to glance to the left and noticed some ancient ruins. Natu-
rally they drew my attention.

As I moved closer to them I saw a person emerge from
the ruins. Although I could not see clearly from a distance
the features of the young Man, I knew instantly who He

was. He was just as I had thought of Him. As He drew closer I saw He had blue eyes and flowing reddish-brown hair. His smile was a half-smile and his eyes twinkled kindly.

He stood for a minute and just looked at me. Then I said, "I've always wanted to shake your hand, dear Jesus."

Without a word He held out His hand. As I shook it I could feel the imprint that the nail had left. Just by touching Him I felt good all over.

After I had shaken His hand, He smiled at me again and disappeared. But I was perfectly satisfied. He had given me no more and no less than what I had asked for. My desire had been fulfilled to the letter.

I told my mother the next morning about this wonderful experience. My remembrance was, "He was the most beautiful man I have ever seen and the most wonderful Friend I have. How I love Him!"

MEDITATION

Simplicity

Dear Lord,

You have cautioned us to remain simple and childlike. "Except ye become as little children . . . ye shall not enter the kingdom of heaven." (Mat. 18:3)

Sometimes I let life become very complicated by adding "extras" to it. I have become burdened with social obligations. The sophisticated way makes childlikeness very difficult. I have been spending time on things that tend to pull me away from my higher purposes. I need more time to relax and get to know You better.

Help me to revise my life and re-focus my purposes on Your will. In this way I can better bless my acquaintances. I can also find fulfillment and joyous satisfaction myself. The simple way is Your way. "Master, let me walk with Thee." Thank You, Lord.

Amen.

CHAPTER 24

HIS PEACE REPLACED MY FEAR

GREATER IS HE THAT IS IN YOU THAN HE THAT IS
IN THE WORLD.

—1 John 4:4

Fear of heights was somewhat of a problem to me as a child. I had tumbled off a high wall in the dark one night at an early age and couldn't forget it easily. When the other children wanted to climb to the highest part of the tree tops, I was clutching timidly to the lower boughs. I resisted mountain climbing and disliked airplane rides. However, this had never burdened me too much until after I was married and had children of my own.

One day I was in a room on the seventeenth floor of a large hotel in New York City. I had stopped for overnight on my way south to attend a friend's wedding. Suddenly, I became aware of the long distance to the ground and I was gripped in a frenzy of terrifying fear. I broke out into a wet sweat; my icy hands shook. As I looked at the window, I was frightened of being in such a high room.

In desperation I threw myself face down on the bed. With every fiber of my being I cried aloud to God: "GOD, HELP ME!"

To my utter astonishment I felt the gentle presence of peace pass through me. It was like a breeze blowing gently through a filmy curtain. The Glorious Presence of my Lord filled me with tranquility. Quiet assurance and well-being replaced the panic and I felt calm within and without.

Throughout the ages God had promised through His prophets that the time would come when the third part of Himself would become known to His people. The promise of the coming of the Holy Comforter (Holy Ghost) was finally fulfilled by our Lord, Jesus Christ. The beloved Son of God came and fulfilled the Holy Ghost. It was this Presence that saved me from the fear of heights. I firmly believe it can heal us of any negation man is heir to in this world.

The Holy Ghost or, as I think of it, the Glorious Presence, is part of the evolutionary plan for man as he evolves God-ward with his free will. You do not need to stay in bondage to fears any more than did I. What God does for one, He will do for all. We are all equally loved by our heavenly Father. The Spirit of God through His Son and by action of the Holy Ghost is present to bring us into true power and authority of the right and good. We are children of God and all we have to do is ASK for help in our mortal problems and it will be given.

I rested in His peace and felt the sweet security of God's love all around me. It enveloped me in a new kind of understanding that was tenderly sweet and permanent. By *quickly uniting* with God I was protected and preserved from all evil. Regarding this I am reminded of the Bible passage that says that "God is able to pull down strongholds and cast down every high thing that exalts itself (fears) against the knowledge of God" (See 2 Cor., Chapter 10). It does not matter what variety of fear we may assume; they are all foes to God's full reign and they must be overcome by giving them to God and refusing to keep them! Jesus Christ is the victor over every worldly fear. When we seek His help we gain a victory also. Gratefully I pass along to you what I learned from experience.

MEDITATION

Peace of Mind

Dear Lord,

How false are my fears and how quickly they vanish when I give them to You. When I am alone and am tempted to become afraid, I know You are here. I ask You to help me, and behold, I am free!

And now today I was again tempted to be afraid. I reached out quickly for Your hand as I walked along that city sidewalk. How quickly, it seemed, You took my hand and my racing heart became quiet and calm. The dizziness passed and I regained my composure.

A dark room is like fears. When I turn on the light in the room, the darkness vanishes. Fears vanish when I turn on the light of Your presence. I do not have to go into the dark room and battle the darkness. This does not get rid of the dark. It is only as I turn on the light that its false power vanishes and I realize the dark was only an ABSENCE of Your light and love.

Help me to keep the room of my thoughts filled with Your light and love. O Glorious Presence, infiltrate every crevice and closet of my soul so that I will fear no more. Erase my mortal weaknesses and bring me into the full realization of wholeness and peace forever.

Peace! Peace! Peace, I hear You say. Yes, Lord, I accept Your peace right now! Thank You, dear Lord.

Amen.

CHAPTER 25

THE DIVINE DESTINY OF THE UNITED STATES OF AMERICA

IF YE WILL OBEY MY VOICE INDEED, AND KEEP MY COVENANT, THEN YE SHALL BE A PECULIAR TREASURE UNTO ME ABOVE ALL PEOPLE: FOR ALL THE EARTH IS MINE!

—Exodus 19:5

Have you ever heard of two separate people dreaming the *same* dream on the *same* night? Two people in our big camp had been given the same vision on the same night and one of these people happpened to be me! The other person was a friend, Dr. Frank Laubach, a man for whom I have great respect, both for his fine spiritual leadership and also for his gift of bringing literacy to millions in this world.

Frank was located at the other end of the camp but when we happened to greet each other before breakfast we exchanged experiences. Over a hundred people were at the breakfast table on the morning I first told the C.F.O. (Camps Farthest Out) camp meeting about the experience I am about to recount to you.

Interestingly enough, the Lord knew I was an artist—so I remembered the picture in detail. The Lord also knew Frank was a word man, and he remembered the words in

U.S. Destiny

M. RUSSELL

detail. In this way the Lord made sure His message for the United States of America got through, without discrepancy!

In the vision we saw Christ Jesus standing on top of the globe. His robes radiated a bright, white light that was fringed with golden tints. He stood with His arms outstretched as though embracing all of mankind.

As we followed His sad and compassionate gaze downward we saw a heart in the center of the U.S. To the right, in the waters of N.Y. harbor stood the Statue of Liberty, holding her light of freedom on high for all the world to see. At the base of the world lay an open Bible from which issued the Flame of Life.

To the left of the Bible knelt multitudes of the world's people, holding out empty cups and bowls, pleading for help from America. They were crying and we heard the hopeless wail go up to heaven: "OUR FATHER IN HEAVEN, WE PRAY THAT YOU SAVE US FROM OURSELVES."

To the right of the Holy Bible, with his hat removed, knelt Uncle Sam, head bowed, also in fervent prayer. Then, from Christ came God's answer:

"IF MY PEOPLE, WHICH ARE CALLED BY MY NAME, SHALL HUMBLE THEMSELVES, AND PRAY, AND SEEK MY FACE, AND TURN FROM THEIR WICKED WAYS; THEN WILL I HEAR FROM HEAVEN, AND WILL FORGIVE THEIR SIN, AND WILL HEAL THEIR LAND." (2 Chronicles 7:14)

With these words, the red heart in the center of the United States began to pulsate. Out from it sprang soft, white rays of divine light that spread far and wide, enveloping the whole earth. It appeared as though a cleansing were taking place in every individual in our nation as well as in the entire world. This activity began by each person making him or her self right with God—casting out unforgiveness, lust, pride, greed, hatred, retaliation, covetousness, power and sin of all kinds. Each person was helping and teaching the other the path of love and righteousness.

Since this obviously was a message from the Lord directed to His people in the United States, I hurriedly painted a picture of this great vision. Frank helped me remember the words exactly and they corresponded with those in the Bible.

This picture has since been made into card form and has found a wide distribution so He did not speak in vain. I later replaced the hurried tempera painting with an oil painting which I feel honors our experience and which is now hung and owned by Arcadia Healing World Prayer ministry.

Many people know of the painting and are praying for the purification of the United States and for the world. I praise and give thanks that God still speaks to His people in voice and vision in these latter days. Let us listen with care and obey His tender warning. God wants no ifs, ands, buts, or maybes, but a hearty, love-filled, willing, YES, LORD— I WILL HUMBLE MYSELF, I WILL TURN TO YOUR WILL FROM THE WAY OF THE WORLD, AND I WILL PRAY AND SEEK THY FACE!

MEDITATION

Divine Destiny

Dear Lord,

You have a plan for my soul, just as You have a use for each nation on earth. I know Your plan is perfect, but You gave me free will to use, to work out Your plan. I have made some mistakes, but God has made good out of them all.

I realize that my every thought and action has building power. I have been building a certain framework for my life experience as surely as a contractor erects steel beams. My building materials differ from his, but they build as surely as his do. It requires great wisdom to build well.

Help me, dear Lord, to seek Your counsel, that I may be a good builder. If there are alterations that I need to make, help me to become aware of them before it is too late. I want to build carefully and well. I want to become aware of my divine destiny and I want to fulfill it.

This will take some concentrated time apart with You, Lord. I welcome this idea. It is nice, going aside like this, and communing with You. I know You have been listening, Lord. Now I will be still and listen to You. Speak, Lord, and make Your purpose known. I am listening . . .

Amen.

CHAPTER 26

LEAVE ALL AND FOLLOW ME

THOUGH I BESTOW ALL MY GOODS TO FEED THE
POOR, AND THOUGH I GIVE MY BODY TO BE
BURNED, AND HAVE NOT CHARITY, IT PROFITETH
ME NOTHING. . . . AND NOW ABIDETH FAITH,
HOPE, CHARITY, THESE THREE: BUT THE GREATEST
OF THESE IS CHARITY.

—1 Corinthians 13:3,13

If you have ever been out of work, you will understand
the terrible struggle my cousin had. He had been out of
work for months and was very discouraged. Every job he
applied for was given to someone else just before he got
there. This was in the days when government help was
not thought of. Each man was taught to be responsible
for standing on his own two feet.

I was praying with them every time I visited them and
took them groceries, but I couldn't help his despondency.
Since they were some sixty miles away, I usually tried to
drive over once a week. As I look back on it, it is interesting
to see how God made good out of their seeming impasse.
He always does if we seek His counsel and obey it after
we get it.

The worldly way can be so appealing with its status
symbols of power, prestige, fame, success, money and
greed. How alert we must be to seek God's will for us every

step of the way; otherwise we are taking a swift trip up a dead end street. Self-gain can tint our motives so easily, it seems.

One Saturday when I went to visit them, they were very excited and shared a precious experience with me. My cousin, his wife and daughter were seated at their kitchen table one day that week, discussing his work situation. As I said before, the job offers were few and far between. However, that day he had been offered within the space of four hours, two different positions. Either one of them was his, upon a "Yes."

One job was work in a factory, bottling alcoholic beverages. The other was a caretaker's job for an elderly couple. The factory job paid well. The caretaker's job paid just enough for them to make ends meet. In the caretaker's job he would also have to watch over the elderly couple who were getting feeble.

He would need to do personal odd jobs for them as need arose, such as drive their car and oversee the grounds and property repair. He was almost convinced he would accept the factory job since it was the better paying of the two offers and it offered promotion.

The element of doubt remained, however, as he considered the dire need of the elderly couple. Whatever his decision, it had to be made that day for either job. Thus, the "meeting of the minds" and a call to prayer.

My cousin had no sooner explained the situation to his family and begun to pray when a knock came at their back door. When my cousin rose from his chair to open it, a very old man stood there. His arms were full of bouquets for sale. Although their garden was then in full bloom, it being midsummer, they invited him in for a cup of coffee and some doughnuts. He looked so in need.

He gladly accepted their invitation to step in and rest

awhile, but he declined anything to eat. They soon found that he was a prayerful man and seemed to know the New Testament by heart.

The subject of the two job offers came up and he helpfully pointed out to my cousin how much he was needed by the old folks. The family became involved in such a deep discussion about God and His ways that time passed unnoticed until the visitor closed the conversation. "I should be on my way," he said, "or I will never get my flowers sold."

The family expressed their humble gratitude for his visit. My cousin was so touched by the help he had received regarding a right decision for his new job, he offered him a ride to his destination.

To all this the visitor only smiled and stood up. His figure took on a youthful appearance. His face glowed and his eyes twinkled with a warm smile of parting. Then with a brief bow he stepped out of the door, started toward the corner of the house and disappeared.

They looked for him to pass the window so they could wave but he didn't pass. They ran to the windows on either side of the house and he was nowhere to be seen. They went outside, more than a bit curious. They searched the grounds and the street, but could find no evidence of the visitor anywhere.

When they asked the neighboring villagers who the man was who had been selling flowers, people looked at them oddly and replied, "What man?"

My cousin accepted the position of caretaker and was the source of great comfort for the old folks. Two years afterward, the elderly gentleman passed on. Then the elderly lady needed him more than ever. A year later she went also to her rest.

The entire estate was left to him. Knowing him as I do,

I know neither he nor his wife would have coveted the property. The service he rendered was done out of goodness in his heart. And probably that was why God so generously rewarded him. God works that way!

Some years later my cousin felt called to the Lord's ministry. His wife was in full agreement and helped him get enough of an education so that eventually he became an assistant minister in a city church. Today they are very happy and I see them occasionally. We often remark about their strange and helpful visitor. It does my heart good to see the reward of humble, willing hearts dedicated to serving someone and something other than just themselves. "If any of you lack wisdom, let him ask of God, that giveth to all men liberally." (James 1:5)

MEDITATION

Dedication

Dear Lord,
There is much work to be done for You in this world. You need my dedication. If every so-called Christian were truly dedicated to You we could change the world overnight!

I do not want to be a Christian in name only. I want to be a vital part of Your earthly ministry. You have said the harvest is plenteous, but the laborers are few.

Here and now I give my life and will to You, dear Lord. Take it and use it as You will. Make me Your channel of blessings to others You need to reach. Sanctify me for Your holy purpose. I am Yours, O precious Lord. Bring me into the fullness of Your joy.

Amen.

CHAPTER 27

SAVED FROM SUICIDE IN INDIA

GO YE INTO ALL THE WORLD, AND PREACH THE
GOSPEL TO EVERY CREATURE.

—Mark 16:15

Five A.M. was the hour of decision! Sundar Singh had made a resolution: "If I cannot find peace of mind this night, I shall kill myself. I will lie down on the track and let the train run over me!" The Indian Ludhiana express passed at the bottom of his father's garden so he could do this.

The decision had come after a lifetime battle with depression. He had been born with a torturous longing for peace of mind. An inner restlessness to find "shanti"—that comprehensive Hindi term that means not only peace of mind but complete satisfaction of soul—would not let him go.

Here is an example of a soul, born for reborning—a soul on a quest—a soul called out from amongst them; he would not be denied! No one understood his need. He, alone, must meet his God.

Sundar as a child was raised in the lap of luxury. He was the youngest son of a wealthy landowner in Rampur, in the State of Patiala. He could have anything his heart desired. But all of the wealth in the world could not buy that for which he longed. Peace of mind seemed to elude him.

115

He had been known as "the child who rubbed his forehead on the temple door." He had studied at the feet of Hindu holy men, seeking that treasure of treasures. By the age of seven he could recite the entire Bhagavad-Gita in Sanskrit.

He searched the Granth of the Sikhs at the seashore. He read the Quran of the Muhammadans in the cool Himalayas where the family spent the hot summers. . . . all to no avail.

His mother, interested in the American missionaries, was instrumental in enrolling him in a mission school. Yet when his turn came to read from the Bible he felt an aversion to it. Great pride for the Granth stirred his Sikh blood to deep antagonism. Soon he had become a ringleader of a group of boys bent on hating Christianity. This resulted in his tearing up the New Testament and burning it.

His removal from the mission school to a government school did not gain for him any peace either. As in so many cases, the fault lay not in outer circumstances, but within the individual. Nothing could satisfy the hunger of this famished soul, it seemed. His search led him into many studies, the practice of Yoga being but one. In this he learned how to throw himself into a trance and achieve quietness. But this was only temporary and when he came out of the trance he felt worse than when he had entered!

All of this had taken place before he had even become sixteen. On the night of his decision the young man bathed in Hindu fashion and in desperation found a New Testament and retired to his room. Throughout the night his light burned as he read, meditated and prayed on his knees. "I must have shanti," he whispered, "or I will die." His prayers were long and earnest, and the God of his being stirred within.

How truly our precious Lord promised, "Ye shall seek Me and find Me WHEN ye shall search for Me WITH ALL YOUR HEART." (Jer. 29:13) The words, "all your heart," meant that all deception, all pride, hate, fear, and all negation must be relinquished willingly if the Lord was to be found. Bit by bit those barriers were dropped and Sundar Singh became humbly quiet.

As the hands of the clock moved closer and closer to five o'clock, Sundar became aware of a brilliant light flooding his room. In the midst of the cloud of light stood the radiant figure of Jesus Christ. In loving compassion our Lord looked at him and seemed to be saying: "Why do you oppose Me? I am your Saviour. I died on the cross for YOU. Receive my peace." A great peace entered his soul and he rested.

To the many thousands of troubled souls he later ministered to, Sundar Singh repeated these words over and over again. He was a living testimony of peace. All doubt had vanished. His human bonds dropped as he was lifted into heavenly bliss. The joy was so divine he wanted to remain with God forever. But the Lord called him to remain in the world and minister to others. He spent many hours after that in daily quiet communion with the Lord.

Satan has several main temptations to present to those called of the Lord. The story of this famous man's life is known throughout the world today. It is well known, for instance, that as a boy of sixteen, he took his vow to become a Christian Sadhu. This meant donning the saffron robe and renouncing all other religions and riches, and incurring the anger and hatred of his Hindu relatives. His father, in one last attempt to dissuade his son from what he believed was a terrible mistake, showed him his gold and treasures. He offered them all to him if he would only return again to Hinduism.

Worldly wealth is the temptation all who are "called out" have to meet sooner or later. But the show of riches was no temptation to Sundar. He had learned from experience that riches could not buy him the treasure of priceless value he had received. He was not about to trade it in. He calmly went on his way with the serene resolve to serve Jesus the rest of his earthly days.

By adopting the dress of the Sadhu, all castes and classes of Indian society opened to him. He walked the highways and byways of his native land without knowing where his food or lodging would come from and carrying no money or worldly possessions.

Summer and winter he dressed the same, in the long, flowing orange robe of the ascetic. Crowds followed to hear his message and little children flocked around him to touch his graceful garments. Young and old poured out of their houses to implore healing from his touch.

From village to village he went, carrying only his Bible and giving the words of Jesus to the masses.

Sadhu Sundar Singh traveled not only through India, but walked on into the bitterest wilds of Tibet, that mysterious country where prayer flags flutter in the wind and people spend much time grinding out their prayers on a wheel. There were only foot paths and no roads to follow in that day. Witchcraft, incantations and tests by fire and boiling water were common. Torture and imprisonment were often the daily fare for the Sadhu. He suffered greatly for taking the word of Christ to the people. But in between the trials, converts were won. It was men such as this whom we can thank for opening the land to the light and love of our Saviour, Jesus Christ.

At last the great desire of the Sadhu's heart took place. He visited the Holy Land, and as he was praying in the Garden of Gethsemane, it seemed as though Jesus again appeared to him and requested him to minister to all the world. This was in 1920.

Ways and means immediately opened for him to then visit Egypt, Switzerland, Germany, Sweden, Denmark, Holland, Norway, England and America, speaking and exhorting the people to come closer to Christ and live in a manner pleasing to Him.

In returning to his native land he once more set out for Tibet. As he climbed high into the mountain passes he did not look back. He continued climbing and has not been heard of since. As the Sadhu often said: "The Lord is my helper; I will not fear what men shall do unto me." (Hebrews 13:6)

The ancient land of India has given the Western world much food for thought. Among the unique Indian religious concepts is the idea of renunciation of all worldly pleasure for the eventual absorption into deity. The world will always wonder about the ascetics of India. Their quiet love of the invisible, self-existent One, and their surrender, have been generally incomprehensible to Western thought.

By simple dress and diet they have found life more fulfilling, and when their ideas are blended with Christianity, it makes a powerful combination.

MEDITATION

Witness

Dear Lord,

Make me ever mindful of the needs of others. May I be a strong support to them by fearlessly witnessing to Your great goodness in my own life.

I realize that at times this may be difficult to do. Teach me the right approach each time so that my witnessing may be appreciated and accepted with good will.

Place the right words in my mouth and let Your glory pour forth to the right person, at the right moment, in the right way.

There may be times when I can best witness by being completely silent and just setting a good example. Let me know when to speak and when to be quiet. Let my life be a living witness to You either way, dear Lord.

Amen.

CHAPTER 28

OUR UNFAILING FRIEND

I HAVE CALLED YOU FRIENDS: FOR ALL THINGS
THAT I HAVE HEARD OF MY FATHER I HAVE MADE
KNOWN UNTO YOU. YE HAVE NOT CHOSEN ME,
BUT I HAVE CHOSEN YOU, AND ORDAINED YOU,
THAT YE SHOULD GO AND BRING FORTH FRUIT.
—John 15:15

It has well been said that on a clear day one can see
forever! I like to think this means that one's mind needs to
be uncluttered in order to become aware of eternity.

One afternoon after a busy day, I sat down to meditate
upon God. I let the clutter of the day drop into the
wastebasket and just relaxed every muscle in my tired body.

I was considering the beautiful verse of Scripture where
Jesus was speaking to His friends and calling them His
special friends. Gradually a beautiful vision unfolded
before me.

A little red, dirt road wound gently off through a valley,
then up and over a green-clad hillside. The day was calm,
peaceful and very, very clear. It was the most calm, clear
day I have ever seen. The sky was pastel blue with not
a cloud in sight.

As I was marveling over this calm, peaceful scene my
attention was attracted skyward again. At first I was only

conscious of the blue beauty that seemed almost overwhelming. Then, little by little a figure took shape—Jesus Christ appeared.

At first I saw His beloved face—so full of love and compassion, radiantly beautiful—bearing the most beautiful expression I have ever known. The hair on His head was fine like lamb's wool and it flowed down onto His shoulders.

His body was clad in a shimmering white robe that fell down to His sandaled feet. It was an exquisite experience to behold my Saviour in person. What a Glorious Presence He is!

I expected the vision to fade but I was due for another surprise. Instead of disappearing skyward, He was descending earthward! I was spellbound as He came closer and closer until at last He stretched out his foot and stepped on the earth. He looked into me with a deep tender love. I wanted to cry and laugh for joy, both at the same time! How silently, how silently Christ makes His presence known.

The God I know is not a God on a throne off in the sky somewhere, nor is He an impersonal nobody. He is a God close by. My God is no stranger to me any more. He is the Spirit of the Universe, yes, but He is also personable, friendly and close to me.

I'll always have a Friend—a dear Friend who never wavers in His faithfulness—the Glorious Presence—the Holy Comforter here, with me now and forever, even as Jesus promised. What a difference it makes to know this!

You have the same Friend I have. I am sure of this because God loves us all equally well. What He will be to me, He will be to you also. For this knowledge and for the love that prompts Him to be personal as well as impersonal, I humbly thank Him.

Friendship

Dear Lord,

You know that I have been very lonely. But now I have found You. What a blessing You bring to me, O precious Saviour!

Loneliness is this world's number one malady. If people only knew that they have the most wonderful Friend they could ever wish for, standing right by their side night and day, they would never feel unloved or alone again.

Thank You, dear Saviour, for being my Friend.

Amen.

CHAPTER 29

WHY DO YOU PERSECUTE ME?

HE (JESUS) WAS SEEN OF CEPHAS, THEN OF THE
TWELVE: AFTER THAT, HE WAS SEEN OF ABOVE
FIVE HUNDRED BRETHREN AT ONCE: . . . AFTER
THAT HE WAS SEEN OF JAMES, THEN OF ALL THE
APOSTLES. AND LAST OF ALL HE WAS SEEN OF ME
ALSO.

—1 Corinthians 15:5–8

One of the most authentic historical records of Jesus
Christ's appearing to anyone after His ascension was to the
Apostle Paul who was at that time known as Saul.

Saul, according to the record found in Acts, Chapters
eight and nine of the New Testament, was persecuting the
Christians. He felt very self-righteous in his hatred of
Christians, as he believed Jesus was an impostor.

Saul had stood by and consented that beautiful Stephen
be stoned to death. Stephen's last prayer was for God to forgive his killers. "Saul made havoc of the church, entering
into every house, and haling men and women, committed
them to prison." But all this persecution did not cause the
Christians to forsake their faith in Jesus Christ as their
Saviour. We are told that they were scattered abroad, and
went everywhere preaching the word.

"Saul, still breathing threats of slaughter against the
disciples of the Lord, went to the high priest and asked him

for letters to the synagogues at Damascus.'' He intended to search and find all who were committed to Christ, bind them, and bring them to Jerusalem to be killed.

Saul—the hate-filled, self-righteous judge of his fellow man—was journeying along the road to Damascus. He was no different in some respects from some today who feel justified in hating and persecuting their fellow man for religious variances. They too will need to be taught by God the right way to love God and man.

Slowly his horse plodded along carrying him, together with his small band of companions, near to Damascus. Suddenly, a bright light shone out of heaven and engulfed him. Its power knocked him off his horse and as he groveled in the dirt he heard a man's voice addressing him: ''SAUL, SAUL, WHY PERSECUTEST THOU ME?''

Apparently Jesus appeared to Saul, for later Saul told the Corinthians (1 Corinthians 9:1), ''Am I not an apostle? . . . Have I not SEEN Jesus Christ our Lord?''

Saul wanted to be sure. He asked, ''Who are you, Lord?'' And the Lord said, ''I AM JESUS OF NAZARETH WHOM YOU PERSECUTE.'' No room for doubt was left in Saul's mind. Jesus was no impostor; He was the most holy God in Person. (Acts 22)

Then Saul, trembling and astonished asked, ''Lord, what will you have me do?'' Saul was now beginning to comprehend the serious error of his way. Here we see the compassion of our Lord in full action. He was willing to forgive Saul for his terrible acts and grant him a place in His earthly work and a place in His heavenly kingdom.

Jesus replied: ''ARISE, AND GO INTO DAMASCUS: AND THERE IT SHALL BE TOLD YOU OF ALL THINGS WHICH ARE APPOINTED FOR YOU TO DO.'' Saul went on to report that he was blinded by the heavenly vision. Because he could not see, he groped his way to the city, with others leading him by the hand. Can you imagine a more humbling experience?

Saul learned a valuable lesson which he repeated over and over again as he ministered in the Lord's service. To the Romans he said of the Lord, "Every knee shall bow . . . and every tongue shall confess to God." (Rom. 14:11) For God is able to pull down strongholds and cast down "every high thing that exalts itself against the knowledge of God, bringing into captivity every thought to the obedience of Christ." (2 Cor. 10:5) Again, to the Romans he warned, "Be not wise in your own conceits!"

Saul, formerly filled with bitter judgment of others, humbly came to know there is but one judge of man and it was not he. He later addressed the Athenians and told them that God "has appointed a day, in which *he* will judge the world." (Acts 17:31)

The rest of the account tells us that Saul went as he was instructed to the house of Judas and was blind for three days, and "neither ate nor drank." Then the Lord appeared in a vision to one of His faithful followers in that city by the name of Ananias. He told him where Saul was and to go to him and lay hands on him and pray so that Saul might regain his sight.

Ananias questioned the Lord, saying that Saul had an evil reputation and was in the city for the purpose of killing people like himself. But the Lord explained to Ananias that He knew all about it and that He could use Saul in a very special way. He could send him to tell the Gentiles that Jesus was Christ and Lord.

Ananias did as he was told and Saul received his sight. "Straightway he preached Christ in the synagogues, that he is the Son of God." (Acts 9:20)

MEDITATION

Humility

Dear Lord,

I know I'm no good to myself or You unless I am humble. I have felt superior to others for quite some time now. Pare me down to size, Lord. I know it's not good to be proud and self-righteous.

If You had judged me as harshly as I have judged some others I know I wouldn't stand a chance of ever making it. Forgive me, Lord. When I persecute others, I persecute You. I don't want to do that, Lord.

Help me to stop judging others. If someone attends a certain church, may I not judge or condemn them. You are in charge of them even as You are in charge of me. If a person's skin color differs from mine, may I find beauty in it. Help me to leave all judgment to You and to look to You for true discernment in a situation.

I would be kind to others and appreciate them for whatever they are. Help me see the Christ in them, even as I know You are in me. Help me to let others be themselves and not try to re-make them.

Stop me, Lord, if I begin to judge or condemn others whose views differ from mine in any way. Remove this unChristlike habit from me. If there is any hate in me, take it all away. Fill me with Your love, dear Lord. I humbly ask this.

Amen.

CHAPTER 30

THROUGH THE EYES
OF AN ARTIST

THE COMFORTER, WHICH IS THE HOLY GHOST,
WHOM THE FATHER WILL SEND IN MY NAME, HE
SHALL TEACH YOU ALL THINGS AND BRING ALL
THINGS TO YOUR REMEMBRANCE, WHATSOEVER
I HAVE SAID UNTO YOU.

—John 14:26

Many people come to the little studio my husband built
in our back yard. They talk with me, see my pictures and
frequently offer to buy them. Yet I have had only one
formal art lesson in all the years I have been painting.
The Scripture tells us to look to the Lord, and "I will
instruct thee and teach thee." (Ps. 32:8)

This is exactly what I have done. Jesus Christ has been my
constant art instructor. It is a remarkable companionship
that we have—Jesus and I. Every day I become quiet and
commune with Him. Listening intently as Jesus sweetly
directs each picture, I then go to my easel and try to follow
His instructions.

One day something special happened that I will share
with you. I'm sure this will amuse you even as it did me.
I decided to attempt a painting of "Him whom my soul
loveth." Of course, I felt it should look as authentic as

possible. So I strove to paint the picture as nearly as I thought Jesus might have looked.

I made His eyes blue, like my own son's eyes. I painted His hair dark brown, like my husband's hair. I clothed Him in the garb of His day.

When I finished and stepped back to look, I must admit I was quite impressed by what I saw. It was an excellent picture and I thought of my many friends who would compliment me on it. I laid my brush down and went to my couch to commune with Jesus.

I asked Him if He liked His portrait. I also asked if He thought His portrait would be an inspiration to others. Of course, my one desire was to please Him. But frankly, I thought I had done a pretty good job.

I shall never forget my chagrin as I listened to my Instructor's reply. He certainly has a way of paring down our ego! The message seemed to be this: "You have worked diligently, dear child. But if you want your painting true to the way I looked when I walked the hills of Galilee you will need to make a few changes:

MY EYES WERE BLUE—LIKE THE CORNFLOWER. MY HAIR WAS THE COLOR OF RIPENED WHEAT. AND REMOVE THE FLOWERS FROM IN FRONT OF MY FEET: I WILL HAVE NOTHING BETWEEN ME AND MY PEOPLE."

Well, I got up in a hurry and went back to my canvas and humbly corrected my mistakes! My Instructor had spoken and, rest assured, I was His humble, obedient and willing student.

When the painting was finished it was a real joy to know that my picture was now a first-class likeness of my dear Teacher—a Teacher very presently living among us, here and now. Thank You, beloved Jesus.

MEDITATION

Receptivity

Dear Lord,

If I had a million dollars in the bank and never went near the place, it wouldn't do me very much good. This wonderful artist has told us You were her instructor. I have seen her work and it is good! You were her rich resource and she knew it and humbly sought Your instruction and benefited not only herself but those who enjoy her paintings.

The Bible tells us that God's supply of goodness is inexhaustible. It is never-ceasing and eternal. This is much like a vast bank account for me. I can come to You, Lord, and receive whatever I need.

Increase my receptivity and keep me humble, Lord. Thank You.

Amen.

CHAPTER 31

FAITHFULNESS TO GOD IS REWARDED

HE THAT IS FAITHFUL IN THAT WHICH IS LEAST IS FAITHFUL ALSO IN MUCH.

—Luke 16:10

Living close to God's will is the most fulfilling experience anyone can have. I love Him and I love His Holy Word, the Bible. Because of this, I have memorized a number of Bible passages—some of my favorites—and I find them very handy, especially in times of emergency.

Some of the helpful passages are the following:

"BE STILL AND KNOW THAT I AM GOD!"

"I WILL BE EXALTED IN THE EARTH."

"GOD IS OUR REFUGE AND STRENGTH, A VERY PRESENT HELP IN TROUBLE."

"I CAN DO ALL THINGS THROUGH CHRIST THAT STRENGTHENETH ME."

"GREATER IS HE THAT IS IN YOU, THAN HE THAT IS IN THE WORLD."

There are other passages I use, too. For instance, when neighbors gossip about reports of war, riots or epidemics I repeat to myself some of the promises of God and I am strengthened. Surely God is good and God will take care of His children IF WE TRUST HIM.

Knowing this from experience in many ways, I have found living for God is not only a privilege, but a very great pleasure. In this way all the good possible in any situation always comes to me. God IS a good God!

As a young woman, living in a small midwestern town in America, I was faithful to God's Spirit directing me from within. I was careful to follow God's direction. Because of this faithfulness, a strange and wonderful blessing was received.

One day I was out walking. Our house was on the south side of the town and there was a high hill there. At the base of the hill there was a country road and the railroad track wound between the road and the edge of the river. It was as I was walking west along this country road that a vision appeared to me. I became conscious of a tall man walking east on the railroad track. As he approached, I watched, and a great hush fell over the earth and air. I seemed to be the only living creature in that vast open area.

I did not feel the slightest fear as he seemed to disappear, but I was moved to look upward. There, in the west, I saw dark clouds rising above the horizon. These were joined by somewhat lighter ones as they kept rising higher until they were high above the hill. As I continued looking, Christ Jesus stepped out through the clouds, clothed in robes of rich purple shades. This vision was beyond description.

The majesty of His presence—the beauty of His garments—the moving clouds—the grandeur of it all created an atmosphere in which I lived and moved for days afterward.

I shall always be grateful to our heavenly Father for the revelation of His Son in this beautiful vision. It is the only one I have ever had, but it is still an inspiration to me these many years. I am now sixty. It is still vivid in my memory.

"OUT OF ZION, THE PERFECTION OF BEAUTY, GOD HATH SHINED." (Ps. 50:2) God has promised that we who seek the kingdom first will receive the good things in life. This has been my experience. God's promises are true and I thank Him daily.

MEDITATION

Reward

Dear Lord,

So often it seems the good people of this world go without reward. It doesn't seem fair I wonder how You feel about this? Perhaps I am judging ignorantly. Possibly these good people are receiving rewards that are not apparent to worldly view.

You are the true judge so I had better leave this kind of thinking to You and be content in doing what is right and good. The reward will follow in the right way, the way I need it. Your promises are sure.

You have told us to seek the kingdom of God first and His righteousness; and all things shall be added. Lord, help me to love God more than I love myself. This seems hard to do. Guide and encourage me to serve and help others in some definite way I have not thought of before. Help me to serve You not for the reward, but for the joy of serving and the blessed assurance of God's Holy Spirit with me.

Open my awareness to new horizons of action and open my door to the blessings of fruitful living. And thank You, Lord, for all the goodness that pours daily into my life. I love the good life!

Amen.

CHAPTER 32

DENY SICKNESS!

AWAKE THOU THAT SLEEPEST, AND ARISE FROM
THE DEAD, AND CHRIST SHALL GIVE THEE LIGHT!
—Ephesians 5:14

I want to share what seems to me to be the most wonderful experience in my life. We hear of people who are sick and we kindly tell them, "Yes, I know just how you are feeling." But until we are sick ourselves, we really do not understand how much they suffer.

I was quite a healthy person and seldom was sick until I caught what is known as "sleeping sickness." I wanted to sleep all the time. I was asleep as I tried to walk around and I could hardly wake up to eat. I finally went to bed, and if it had not been for my good, kind family who forced food into my mouth, I would have starved to death. My friends were wonderful and took turns staying with me, although at the time I was not too aware of my husband, children, friends, or anything but my desperate desire to sleep.

One night I was roused by a strange feeling. I sensed that everyone had gone to bed and yet I heard a voice speaking my name. It was a man's voice but it was not my husband or anyone I recognized. He kept speaking until I was roused by curiosity. I made a supreme effort to see who was standing by my bed. It was someone who loved me, I could tell. It was a wonderful voice; it didn't sound like any of my friends or acquaintances, yet I felt a great love reaching me. So I opened one eye and looked. There was no one there!

As I considered this both eyes flew open in astonishment. I realized it must be the voice of the Lord, Jesus Christ. I almost stopped breathing to listen to what was being said to me!

He told me to deny sickness and to deny anything that was not good. He told me He would help me think about God's wonderful gift of good life which was never sick. He reminded me of how good God is and how much God loves me. Then He softly and gently said, "You are made whole!"

Oh, that wonderful Voice! And those wonderful words He told me! I shall never forget it as long as I live.

Soon I felt strength coming into my mind and body and I continued to deny sickness by saying, "Sickness does not belong to me; God never made it. Sickness doesn't have any power over me. I belong to God. God is good. Life is good! My help comes from God, Who is present through Jesus Christ. Jesus said, 'I am the way!' Jesus Christ helps me with His tremendous overcoming power. Praise God that God is all-powerful and He loves me!"

Oh, how grateful I am to know this—really KNOW this. God is so good!

By morning I felt so much better I made the effort to get out of bed, and in several days I was up and around. I continued to improve until, by God's grace and mercy, the sickness was completely overcome. I understand this is a rare case of healing, but by the love of the Glorious Presence I am whole and well today.

Denial

Dear Lord,

I remember when You were in the wilderness and You were tempted by Satan. You denied him three times and then he left You. I can see how false and temporary negation is. I have been tempted many times but when I stand firm and deny error in those first three or four seconds, the temptation leaves me!

I am referring to moral issues, Lord. Now I realize from Your teaching that I have a right to deny sickness, too. It does not belong to me or to any of God's people. I will simply put Your powerful name in my denial and say something like this:

"BY THE POWER AND AUTHORITY OF JESUS CHRIST, GET THEE HENCE, ERROR!" Or I might say, "BY THE POWER AND BLOOD OF JESUS CHRIST, NEGATION HAS *NO* POWER OVER ME!"

I also understand I have a right to deny poverty or want of any kind. Neither does it have any power over me to make me weak or afraid because I belong to God!

Help me to stand firm and deny lack, Lord. Lend Your power when I deny it: "BY THE POWER AND AUTHORITY OF JESUS CHRIST I DENY LACK. GOD SUPPLIES FOR ALL MY NEEDS ABUNDANTLY. I OPEN MY EYES AND EARS AND HEART AND FIND MY SUPPLY *NOW*. THANK YOU, GOD!"

Amen.

CHAPTER 33

I WAS AN AGNOSTIC BUT—

DID NOT OUR HEART BURN WITHIN US WHILE HE
TALKED WITH US BY THE WAY, AND WHILE HE
OPENED TO US THE SCRIPTURE?

—Luke 24:32

There was a time in my life when I was estranged from
God and disillusioned with the world. Either direction I
looked seemed hopeless. I believed Jesus was just a historical
figure, or even a myth and that the Bible had been written
by opinionated men, some wise, some very unwise. In other
words, I was part of a large body of agnostics. The future,
under those circumstances, did not look very bright.

Perhaps this is not too uncommon today. People get
wrapped up in this life of worldly pleasure. Or perhaps they
have an unpleasant church experience, or have failed in the
business world and have grown sour against everyone and
everything.

Sometimes people have a wonderful religious experience
and make the mistake of sharing it, only to have some
religious leader or advocate of some organized religion
criticize them for it. It is sad that so many people feel
so perfect that they can condemn their fellow man without
knowing them, or judge a particular philosophy by the
people who follow it.

I had such an experience. A certain religious group

appealed to me for the philosophy they taught. But as I got involved with a few of the folks who attended the meetings I found great discrepancies in their habits. They talked one thing and lived another. Because of this I condemned the whole philosophy and left the group. Since then I have come to see the folly of judging a particular teaching by a certain few who may interpret it correctly or incorrectly.

At the time when I was an agnostic I was depressed. I searched for some form of hope aside from organized religion that would give me direction and a happy sense of fulfillment. I remember reading some of the teachings of Buddha, Krishna, Lao-tse, and a smattering of Yoga. There were certain aspects of all these that seemed appealing, but I was in no way satisfied. Life seemed so useless.

One night I was considering the man, Jesus, supposed to be the Messiah. Could He be real as the Bible claimed? The more I contemplated this, the more a desire welled up within me that yearned for the truth of the whole matter. Were all the promises of so many people—the prophecies— the preparations for His coming over centuries preceding His supposed birth—were all these false? The more I considered it, the more I demanded an answer.

Why, I asked myself, would so many people want to deliberately try to deceive others? Perhaps they were self-deceived, I thought. I reread certain texts. There I found definite witness to lives changed and courage that exceeded normal human limits.

If so many people seemed healed, as the New Testament reported, then there must have been a very great multitude trying to deceive others. Why should so many do this, I wondered? Surely they would have no gain *except ridicule* from testifying as a false witness.

Various scenes flashed through my mind: Jesus, healing Peter's mother-in-law, and she rose from her bed and

ministered to them (certainly, if she had faked her healing it would have been quickly discovered and Peter would not have been one of Jesus' staunch followers); Jesus, healing the centurion's servant at a distance, only by His spoken word. Jesus, healing the woman with the bloody issue; Jesus, cleansing the lepers; Jesus, healing the man who was possessed; Jesus, taking Jairus' dead daughter by the hand and, as reported in Mark 5:42, "straightway the damsel arose, and walked: for she was of the age of twelve years. And they were astonished with a great astonishment." And what about the raising to life of Lazarus after having been embalmed in the tomb for three days? The reports went on and on.

Without realizing it, something began to happen to me and it was to be the greatest thing that had ever happened in my life! At that time I did not know it.

Slowly, while in this contemplative mood, the world slipped from view. I seemed to merge into the center of my being, into a very holy, pure place. And then, before my astonished eyes there burst forth a radiant sphere of purplish-blue light. As I looked into the center of this Godly radiance, I heard a mighty roaring like that of a mighty waterfall.

As the sound died away into a void the blue light got brighter and lighter until it burst into a dazzling white light with a lovely golden fringe. The light then seemed to fan out and encompass the whole universe and I was a part of it. Its beauty and peace filled my soul with ecstasy. What joy—what love I felt!

Then into the middle of this beautiful light there quietly appeared the arms, shoulders and head of a man—a great Being of Light. I knew it to be the presence of Jesus, radiant with the Christ light.

His whole being was in lifelike colors. All of His features

were strong and evenly balanced with a beautiful symmetry of line. The hair was light, reddish brown, the eyes were blue and held a heavenly twinkle. A friendly smile played upon His full, expressive lips. There was a look of kindness, tenderness, love, compassion and understanding in His beautiful face.

Without any words spoken, I seemed to understand the meaning of His presence. I felt intuitively the message that He wanted me to have was in part this:

"NOW, I HAVE COME AGAIN. NOW YOU KNOW THAT I AM JESUS, THE CHRIST WHO COMES TO YOU FOR THE WITNESS OF THE TRUTH. I AM WITH YOU ALWAYS. CALL UPON ME AND I WILL MINISTER TO YOU QUICKLY AND TO ALL THOSE FOR WHOM YOU ASK IN LOVE. WHEN YOU NEED ME PLEASE CALL UPON MY NAME AND YOU WILL COME TO UNDER-STAND ALL THINGS."

There was a pause and then He seemed to say, "RECEIVE YE MY LOVE."

The vision cleared away leaving me filled with such a tender, intense sense of light and love as I had never known before. His love thrilled me to the core. The light that had been given me illumined my thoughts, and I found I could understand many things in the Bible that had before been obscure. Truth began to unfold for me like a flower upon a dry desert. I found peace of mind and a goal in life, hope for the future and blessed happiness in my Lord and Saviour, Jesus Christ.

The Bible is right: "With thee is the fountain of life; in thy light shall we see light!" (Ps. 36:9) Jesus Christ illumined me. Now I know without doubt, Jesus lived, Jesus taught, Jesus healed, Jesus died and resurrected, and Jesus is the Son of God. He is real, and He lives! Praise His holy name!

141

Illumination

Dear Lord,

You are the light of the world. In Your beautiful light I behold light never ceasing, forever shining to illumine the universe and to illumine the minds of men.

Grant me an ever-increasing awareness of light as I daily meditate upon God. You truly are my Lord. "The Lord is my light and my salvation!" Your light is here, dear Lord. May all Your earth children see it and know You are real.

There are many today who are agnostics. I pray especially for them, that they may search to find the truth. Every sincere seeker is rewarded in the way that is right for him. Thank You for answering my need and giving me assurance of eternal life.

Amen.

CHAPTER 34

ETERNAL LOVE

I KNOW THAT MY REDEEMER LIVETH, AND THAT
HE SHALL STAND AT THE LATTER DAY UPON THE
EARTH.

—Job 19:25

I had beseeched God; I had blamed God; I had prayed
all to no avail! It seemed my condition was becoming
hopelessly worse instead of better.

Why don't you try exercise, a well-meaning friend
queried? (I could hardly get out of bed to go to the
bathroom.) Why don't you try chanting, another friend
asked? Someone suggested I go to his church and be healed.
Why not try Christian Science? Why not do this or that—
or the other thing? Had I tried this medicine? Had I gone
to that health resort? The list went on and on. I will say,
I tried them ALL—and nothing worked.

I had had major surgery and for months had hardly been
able to muster sufficient strength to live. Months dragged
on to a year and despondency set in—that old tool of the
adversary. Medications mounted until they filled three
shelves of our coat closet, and the doctor ceased his house
calls.

The day finally arrived when I decided I could go no
further. Then and there I humbly requested God to take me

home. I was no good to myself and no good to anyone else on earth. "Just take me, God," I whispered.

You may be able to imagine my great astonishment when a radiant light streamed into my awareness, lifting me into such bliss as this world has never known. This state of love-filled radiance lasted for hours. The glory and grandeur of God's presence was everywhere. I was taught many, many things and knew God to be all in all.

When I regained consciousness I realized I had perfect health, peace, and wonderful eyesight. I took off my glasses and when the eye doctor tested my eyes he reported 20-20 vision. He could not explain it, nor could my medical doctor explain my recovery.

I went to the clothes closet with a bushel basket and filled it with the bottles and boxes of pills. Another basket was filled and carried to the dump. The freedom and gladness and gratitude I had knew no bounds! I wanted to share with the whole world what had happened to me. I felt called to become God's minister. "God has illumined me," I announced to my startled family.

"Are you sure you haven't lost your mind?" they questioned. "Judge the tree by its fruit," I replied. No one could deny that the fruit was indeed very good. I had been healed!

In the next few years I entered training school for the ministry. After several years I prepared to graduate. All this time I had thoughtlessly believed I had gone to God directly, without help from anyone. I was about to receive a graduation surprise.

The day before my graduation exercises was a lovely day. I spent much of the day with friends and finished our visit by a walk in the woodland near my dormitory. As we parted company until later, I silently gave thanks for the beauty of the day.

It was twilight. The mourning doves and other birds were peacefully singing their last evening carols. There seemed to be a hush on the air. A feeling of holiness swept over me and I sensed the Presence of a Being standing beside me.

Turning to the left, I was spellbound by the fact that I was looking directly into the love-filled face of Jesus Christ. He was gazing down at me with such tenderness and loving intimacy, my heart stood still! His eyes gazed deep into my soul. I knew He knew all, and—UNDERSTOOD. Tenderly He caressed me with His eyes and I was enchanted. I adored Him.

Never had I ever known a man like this one. The man of all men, the man, Jesus the Christ. He won me completely—mind, body and soul! And He won me PERMANENTLY.

I was given to know that all the goodness of God that I had received was due to His being the door—the perfect transmitter of divinity in this world. "No man cometh unto the Father, but by me." (John 14:6)

God's light is absolute, but Jesus' love makes it relative. He came, a light unto the world, the Christ in the flesh. He suffered the bitter brutality and hatred of men so that He could help us by becoming the Mediator between God and man. Can you comprehend such love? Jesus Christ IS love personified. This surprising experience taught me this.

It has been many years since I graduated and went into the field of service for God. I can truthfully say I never would have been able to sustain a ministry and keep my faith, and have the compassion I needed to serve, had I not known our Lord and Saviour, Jesus Christ. Knowing Him has made the difference between success and total failure.

The fruits of my ministry have been abundant. It is easy

to tell what ministers know our Lord and those who are faking their relationship. All I can advise is that they seek humbly and sincerely, and they, too, will find their reward. The greatest love in the universe awaits our awareness and our gratitude.

Divine Love

Dear Lord,

Your love reaches out and enfolds me. Your love permeates my being. Your love wraps me in a mantle of light and I am safe and secure forever. Your love draws me higher in God-awareness. Your love brings me into oneness and harmony with my fellow man.

Your love strengthens and protects me in time of trial and temptation. Your love comforts and advises me. Your love smooths away difficulties and renews my spirit.

Your love tenderly heals me. Your love quietly provides for my every need. Your love shares Your ideas with me. Your love is measureless and forever. I am humbly grateful!

Now I know what the Apostle Paul meant when he asked: "Who shall separate us from the love of Christ? Shall tribulation, or distress, or persecution, or famine, or nakedness, or peril, or sword? I am persuaded, that neither death, nor life, nor angels, nor principalities, nor powers, nor things present, nor things to come, nor height, nor depth, nor any other creature shall be able to separate us from the love of God." (Romans 8)

All else will vanish, dear Lord, but Your Love will remain forever. Thank You, Lord, for loving me.

Amen.

CHAPTER 35

AS SAFE AS IN JESUS' POCKET

THE LORD GOD IS A SUN AND SHIELD: THE LORD
WILL GIVE GRACE AND GLORY: NO GOOD THING
WILL HE WITHHOLD FROM THEM THAT WALK
UPRIGHTLY.

—Psalm 84:11

It was a dream, a very vivid dream in color. I want to
tell you about it because I feel it was more than just a
dream—it was a prophecy. Often God teaches us in our
unconscious state.

Most of the time we awake and never remember it. But
this was one time that I did remember. And I shall always
remember it and hold it close to my heart as God's promise
to those who love Him. I will tell it in first person so
you may be with me in the experience.

The location is my home and the area surrounding my
home. I am looking out of the window and suddenly I
see great desolation taking place, yet my home is left intact
and those within my home are unhurt.

As I stand wondering how or why all this happened, a
great, rushing wind comes and, like a giant hand, picks up
the entire house. I am not afraid. For a while, it seems, we
travel through space. I am peaceful and feel as safe as
though I were in Jesus' pocket.

We land—but where? I do not know. My surroundings

are heavenly. I behold beautiful foliage and flowers, stately trees and a path. A great peace enfolds all.

I see people walking ahead of me on this path—each going forward. Each person is walking alone. I hurry to catch up to the nearest one, then touch him on the shoulder. "Where are we?" I ask.

He turns and smiles and I notice that he is of a different race and color than I. But he does not speak, nor does he answer my question. He keeps on walking.

I catch up with and touch another person and ask the same question. As he turns I again note that he is of still another race and color. He, too, does not speak nor answer my question, but turns and continues to go forward. In my quest I reach and touch several people; each one is different and quite individual. But no one speaks and no one answers my question.

Then I hear the voice, a loud voice which fills all the atmosphere. "NONE BUT THE PURE IN HEART CAN REMAIN HERE." The voice keeps repeating this message: "None but the pure in heart can remain here. None but the pure in heart can remain here."

I awoke in the morning with a sense of awe which stayed with me for days. And I knew that the dream had a very special message: that I and those with me and those who depend on God will be safe—no matter what happens to the world.

Jesus Christ said, "I am with you, even to the end of the world." I believe Him. God's power is always over those who love Him and preserves them for His own. We are as safe as though we were in Jesus' pocket.

MEDITATION

Safety

Dear Lord,

I must admit I have felt a bit uneasy lately over all the talk about the end of the world. You know I have lived a pretty good life in that I try to please God most of the time.

Now I am wondering if more is required of me. I ask You to lead me into relationships that will help me increase my spiritual awareness. Show me how to share my talents and abilities with others on a selfless service basis. I feel these are days of great opportunity and I may have been missing out on a lot. Open my eyes and ears to receive the lessons You want to teach me and illumine my understanding so that I and my household will be safe with You. You are the only way into eternal life; there is no other way. I trust You, Lord; help me to be receptive to Your leadings. Thank You, dear Saviour.

Amen.

CHAPTER 36

SHARING IS CARING

IF ANY MAN HEAR MY VOICE AND OPEN THE DOOR,
I WILL COME IN TO HIM, AND WILL SUP WITH HIM,
AND HE WITH ME.

—Revelation 3:20

"And the Lord just—DISAPPEARED!" my friend ended limply. She gave me a helpless look. This was part of an affidavited report in her organization's records as well as public knowledge. We both knew the man who had testified by witness before a notary on this. He was a well-respected businessman of the community. "Tell the story to me again," I encouraged, and she did so.

Here is the report. A friendly businessman was hastening home after work to his bachelor apartment in the heart of a busy city. It was a rainy, spring day. As he splashed along through the rain, tilting his large umbrella against the gusts of wind, he suddenly bumped into a man walking in the same direction.

"Oh, excuse me," he shouted. Then seeing the other man's smiling response, he hastily invited him to get under his umbrella. The stranger seemed grateful for the shelter and together they hustled along, avoiding as best they could the other passers-by and jumping across the large puddles and rivulets that were forming on the sidewalk. Laughing and commenting they managed quite well as a team.

"Who are you?" the businessman queried. "Do you live around here?" "No," replied the man, "I'm from out of town."

"You surely picked a poor day to be in the city," the businessman laughed in return. "Are you here on business?"

"Yes," replied the stranger. "What church is that across the street?"

"Oh, I don't offhand know," replied the businessman. "I see it's locked up. They probably wouldn't welcome two dripping strangers like us on their nice carpets. Who needs Jesus anyway? We've got God.

"Say, you look drenched! Perhaps you had better stop in at my place and get warmed up before you go on your way. We are here, now."

With that the businessman stepped up onto the doorstep and opened the door to what seemed to be a comfortable foyer. "Come on up to my apartment," he invited. "I'm not the best cook in the world, but a neighbor gave me some lasagna to warm up. Maybe you'd like some before you leave. Or are you in a hurry?"

The stranger accepted his invitation and hiked up the stairs after him. The apartment was not plush, but it was warm and cozy. "Excuse me a moment while I stand this dripping umbrella in the bathtub and then I'll take your coat," he said.

He disappeared and shortly returned to take the stranger's ragged coat. He noticed his suit was badly worn also. Then he entered into a conversation about some of his problems. As they conversed he began to feel a warm glow of gratitude for this new friend. He found him most helpful and many of his problems did not seem that difficult any more. Glancing again at the stranger's ragged suit he made a suggestion.

"Say, while I put the food on to heat why don't you

151

slip into a suit I've had for some time and can't wear? I've been looking for someone about my size to give it to. Perhaps it would fit you." The stranger seemed pleased with the idea and shortly came out of the bathroom smilingly wearing it.

"It just fits!" observed the businessman. "That's great! I'm getting too fat," he chuckled. "I surely am grateful for all that good counsel you just gave me." The stranger demurred, saying he had not helped all that much and that he appreciated such hospitality on such a cold, rainy night away from home.

"Do you do this for every stranger you meet?" he queried.

"No," the businessman admitted. "In fact, I am just beginning to realize I could do a lot more for people than I do.

"Come, let's sit down and eat before the food gets cold."

It had been a habit for the businessman to give thanks to God for the day's blessings and for the food of each meal. Tonight he felt moved to invite his new friend to offer grace.

With heads bowed and eyes closed they entered into a prayer so profound and so beautiful, the businessman was quite impressed. What a man this stranger was! What a good friend he was going to be! How fortunate he was to run into him in the rain! What a rare occasion this was! These and other thoughts flicked through his mind as the communion went on and on—and on.

After some length of time the businessman opened one eye and peeked wonderingly across the table. Seated across from him, at the place he, himself, had set for the stranger, sat the beautiful Christ Jesus—His two hands upturned on the table as He gave the Father thanks. In each hand was the scar of a nail hole.

A stunned silence followed and thoughts whirled as the

businessman's world turned topsy-turvy! Could it be—? Was it possible—? How—? Why—? Questions flooded in without answer.

When he dared to open his eyes again there was no one seated across from him. His own plate rested in front of him untouched and a plate sat across the table from him, untouched—with an empty chair.

No ragged clothing was to be found in the bathroom or indeed anywhere. His suit lay neatly folded, but there was no trace of the Stranger in the apartment, hallway, or down on the sidewalk.

Neighboring tenants were called to search, all to no avail. The Stranger had vanished as suddenly as He had appeared. Had He actually left, or was He standing invisibly by, smiling at the new awareness He had caused? One thing was certain, He had left a remembrance of His presence with a man who had shared what little he had, with Him who has all.

MEDITATION

Sharing

Dear Lord,

Sharing is really caring. When You said, "Freely you have received, freely give," You were speaking right to me! As I read that Bible passage recently and as I have read this wonderful story of the man who shared, I know I have been stingy. Forgive me, Lord.

Others with less than I have are much more generous. Now I intend to change my ways! And today is the day I begin. In fact, as I finish this meditation I have a check made out to a charity in town and I will drive over with it myself.

I know that sharing does not apply to money matters only. I am thinking of a certain family nearby that needs some gardening help. I am also thinking of some friends who have had a lot of trouble and now they have a daughter who could use some help to find peace of mind. I am going calling today, Lord.

Help me to express Your comforting ideas. If we do this together, we will be successful. If I do it on my own, Lord, I will fail.

Help me do these things today and show me tomorrow what I can do to share Your good with others. This is a pretty new experience for me and I'm loving it already! It is quite an adventure—going calling on the neighbors with You! Thank You, Lord.

Amen.

CHAPTER 37

HOW I FOUND JOYOUS FULFILLMENT

YE MUST BE BORN AGAIN. THE WIND BLOWETH
WHERE IT LISTETH AND THOU HEAREST THE SOUND
THEREOF BUT CANST NOT TELL WHENCE IT COMETH
AND WHITHER IT GOETH: SO IS EVERY ONE THAT IS
BORN OF THE SPIRIT.

—John 3:7,8

Everyone, it seems, is born with certain tendencies and capabilities. It appears as though I was born with the strong desire to communicate with God, but try as I would, I never felt I had succeeded. I grew up with the other children in our family and got a job in the mill where my dad worked. Over the years I married and had six children.

Life as a paper-mill worker was not very satisfying. I sought fulfillment through excitement by drinking and traveling with a fast crowd. My dad was a wonderful, hard-working man whom I deeply loved and respected and I am sure I must have caused him many hours of grief.

Over the years many things of a tragic nature happened. My wife's health was not too good and at one point she had seven operations in six years. To date we have buried all but two of our six children. And then, there was my accident.

I was at work in the paper mill when I accidentally stepped on a loose machine belt on the floor. My body was caught up and flung through the air on the end of this belt, then crashed down to the floor. Again and again this happened before someone could get to the huge machine and shut it off.

When they picked me up I had a concussion of the brain; both arms, elbows, knees, legs and ankles were crushed as well as my right hip, and serious abdominal injuries were incurred. They rushed me to the hospital. The priest was summoned and I was conscious enough to realize the last rites were being given. All hope was given up for my recovery.

I did recover, however! With a ball-and-socket hip joint and numerous metal pins and braces, I managed to get going again and returned to work. The pain I suffered daily was almost intolerable and my drinking increased. I wanted to live, but I wondered if the agony was worth it. I sought fulfillment from God deep down inside of me, but I did not know how to get it. So I shouted, bullied, swore, and forced an existence.

Then I received another blow; my dad died. I used to wonder how he could be so good, but now he was gone. Had his goodness mattered to God? He was fairly young; why couldn't he have lived longer and gotten some enjoyment from life? His parental concern for us children had been beautiful, but he had had to work so hard to eke out a living, it didn't seem fair. My heavy heart searched for these answers when I went to church, hoping to get some relief.

One day I was kneeling in front of the altar, rehearsing in my heart all the good things Dad tried to do for me and all the worry I must have given him. The question of why he had to die so soon when he was so good? This troubled me. Where was he? Did God know about his whereabouts? Was God taking care of him?

I looked up at the cross where the symbol of my Saviour hung, and I whispered: "IS MY DAD WITH YOU, LORD?"

You can imagine how startled I was when it seemed as though God's voice answered back loud and clear: "YES!"

I started backward in shock and quickly looked around the church to see if anyone might be playing a trick on me, but I was alone. This made a deep impression on me and I am sure it brought my soul closer to God than I had ever been before.

It was sometime after that, that I became aware that alcohol was becoming a problem in my life. After a time of considering this I was moved to join A.A. Although this part of my life was then improved, I still had the terrible pain to bear in my hip. Finally, I decided to have another new hip put in.

I was on pain relievers when I went in for surgery and apparently the doctors were not fully aware of my condition. More drugs were administered until I became unconscious. More drugs were given to me to try to correct the situation which only added to my difficulties. My condition worsened and I became unconscious for seven days.

I am told that several God-loving people as well as my immediate family were praying for me and apparently this made the difference between life and death. I finally gained consciousness and upon turning my head I saw Jesus standing by my bedside. Then I would doze off and come to.

People came and went, but often I would see Him standing there, reaching out His beloved hand, touching me in a place that needed healing or relief from pain. Then strength and healing would sweep into me as I would release myself to Him.

For the first time in my life I felt true peace. I was being born anew much as Jesus had explained to Nicodemus long ago. Day after day this occurred until I finally regained health and returned to a good job at the mill. I have many opportunities on this new job to help others. My new way of life makes life worth living!

This is the fulfillment I have wanted all my life. This is the communication I have wanted, too. Jesus Christ knew this and was standing patiently by, awaiting my full attention.

This is like a brand-new life! I can't say that everything is peaches and cream, but I can say that with Jesus Christ here I can turn to Him and solve my problems rather quickly. Every time I visit a friend in the hospital, it is the Lord using me, He does the ministering. I can't begin to tell you of the joy I have through this relationship with Him.

Every day brings a new adventure, a new opportunity to serve Him. I am excited because I feel my area of service is increasing and it feels so good to do something for Him and His kingdom. He has been SO good to me!

Meditation

Fulfillment

Dear Lord,

All through the years You have been waiting for me to humbly come to You. I didn't realize it until now! Now it's different. I know You are here with me. I can feel Your presence and I see the little things You do to let me know You are around and You care.

I want our comradeship to increase, Lord. Despite all my foolishness You still love me. Many times I have tried Your patience, but You have never once tried mine!

I will try to keep Your commandments, dear Lord. I know this is one of many ways I can find fulfillment. You did say, and I feel You saying again:

158

"IF YOU KEEP MY COMMANDMENTS, YOU SHALL ABIDE IN MY LOVE ... THESE THINGS HAVE I SPOKEN UNTO YOU, THAT MY JOY MIGHT REMAIN IN YOU, AND THAT YOUR JOY MIGHT BE FULL." (John 15:10,11) That joy, Lord, is the fulfillment, and I become joyous when I stay in union with Your will and follow Your commands. It is so much easier to be good, and so much joy! Thank You, Lord.

Amen.